CONTROL THE BIDDING

Paul Mendelson writes a weekly bridge column for the *Financial Times*. He teaches in London to huge classes, as well as coaching expert students, and is widely-acclaimed as a brilliant teacher. Having learnt bridge at school, he quickly became a successful tournament player and National champion. He now only makes occasional appearances at big bridge tournaments, but is known to all top world players, organising the prestigious *Macallan International Pairs Championship* in London each spring. Two of his previous books are *Bridge for Complete Beginners* and the best-selling *Right Way to Play Bridge,* to which the present volume is an ideal complement for all those who want to improve their success rating at the table.

CONTROL THE BIDDING

THE RIGHT WAY TO SECURE THE BATTLEGROUND IN BRIDGE

Paul Mendelson

ROBINSON

ROBINSON

First published in Great Britain by Colt Books under the title
Paul Mendelson's Guide to the Bidding Battle in 2003

This edition published in 2008 by Robinson

ISBN 978-0-7160-2156-8

Printed and bound in Great Britain by Clays Ltd, St Ives plc

Constable
is an imprint of
Constable & Robinson Ltd
100 Victoria Embankment
London EC4Y 0DY

An Hachette UK Company
www.hachette.co.uk

www.constablerobinson.com

CONTENTS

INTRODUCTION

Bridge is a game about information. You and your partner gather it during the auction and in defence, and you can infer it from the actions, or otherwise, of your opponents – every bid they make, every card they play...

This book is about destroying, or at the very least corrupting, your opponents' communication, and enhancing your own. It is about how to survive the attacks on your sources of information and judge whether to bid on or double the opposition for a fat penalty.

By the end, you will be alert to every last nuance in the auction – and therefore better prepared for the play – because you are thinking about the entire deal – all 52 cards – not just your own hand. You will destroy your opponents' communications and with it their confidence – however genteel your bridge game may be...

In these modern times, when bidding methods are now so accurate, the new battleground is the sustained attack on your opponents' channels of information. It's time to wise up.

Good players are only good because they know how to interpret information. If you hide their sources, they will be forced to guess. And however good they are, they won't guess right all the time. We will examine how you are able to disrupt your opponents' auction – even with the clear minority of points – forcing them to guess and gamble, instead of betting on a certainty.

The next time you contest a part-score, you will be involved in the auction, stealing a making contract, finding a cheap sacrifice, or pressuring your opponents higher to an unsafe level. When a distributional hand occurs, it will be your opponents having to guess what to do at the four or five level, not you.

You will find that the sheer dynamics of being involved

in many more auctions very exciting. You will feel that
you have really tested your opponents and, when you
come out on top – as I expect you to do – the feeling of
satisfaction will be great. You will still have had your
triumphs, and made the most of your opponents' misfortunes. But, the active element is that you will have been
responsible for your opponents' misfortunes!

If this all sounds a bit aggressive, I can assure you that
there is no conflict between being a charming and delight-
ful character at the bridge table, and a terrier-like player
who hunts down every last chance to win. Whether you
are a masterpoint hunter attending regular congresses, or
an afternoon rubber bridge player for whom the cards are
just a good excuse for a decent tea, you will find that
increased knowledge brings even greater enjoyment of the
game.

In Part One, "Principles of Competitive Bidding", we will
look at the theories which underpin all competitive
situations, so that you understand the dynamics of competition and your bidding style becomes aggressive and
pro-active, but not reckless.

In Part Two, "Competitive Bidding", we will apply these
principles in all areas of the auction, even into the defence
– looking at helping your partner to find the killing lead.
We will discover how to cope with this same aggression
when we face it from other good players. Because one
thing is sure, whenever you encounter good bridge players, they will be as determined as you to make life difficult
for their opponents . . . You will be ready.

Part Three, "Strengthening Your System", concerns the
additions to your convention card which could transform
your results, making you a feared player or pair. Even if
you are a rubber bridge player who, until now, has been
fearful of conventions, I think you will find the sheer logic

of these innovations compelling – and by adopting them with a regular partner or group, you will have a substantial edge over your opponents. They will soon want to catch up with you, and the standard of the whole game will improve dramatically.

Some of these innovations, like Weak 2 bids, and the Advanced Responses to a 2C opening bid, are so logical that they will soon be part of the basic system.

Weak Two Openers, Transfers with advanced responses, and Negative doubles are all featured. Each either produces a competitive edge, or increases the accuracy of your auction to combat competition.

The title of Part Four, "Slam Bidding", speaks for itself. Whilst slam auctions are not often competitive – although opponents' interference is dealt with – good high level bidding is vital to partnership confidence. Roman Key Card Blackwood – a wonderful version of old-fashioned Blackwood – and Cue-bidding should be the mainstays of your slam bidding system. A full knowledge of Quantitative bidding, and other gadgets favoured by the experts will also prove useful.

Finally, Part Five, "High Level Competitive Bidding", deals with the four, five and six level decisions which are increasingly a regular occurrence in tournament bridge and good club bridge.

In all forms of the game, where the players are of a good standard, you will be set high level bidding problems. This section endeavours to help you to make the winning decision.

You may already have an inkling about some of these bidding situations and new conventions. But, only when you and your partner fully understand them will they truly be valuable to you. Indeed, playing a half-learnt system is worse than playing none at all. It ruins your results and destroys your confidence and, worst of all, it encourages your opponents. Having absorbed the contents of these chapters, I guarantee that you will be a stronger player.

Whoever you are playing against, whatever the form of the game you are playing, I am determined that you should have an edge. It is an upward spiral. As you start to have good results against players you thought were better than you, your confidence will grow – theirs will falter. As other players regard you more highly, your results will improve, because they will be afraid of you. But, in the first instance, you must be fearless. The better your opponents, the more aggressive you should be.

I hope that you enjoy what follows. One thing is certain. If I meet you at the bridge table, and you tell me you have read this book, it will worry me. I will know that you have the weapons at your disposal to attack me, and the defences to cope with my attack. I will smile, but I will be fearful. Then again, you will know enough to be fearful too...

Paul Mendelson

PART ONE
PRINCIPLES OF
COMPETITIVE BIDDING

C OMPETITIVE bidding has always been tough, and now it just got tougher . . .

Good players have come to appreciate that an aggressive style will reap long term rewards. Opponents will be barraged too high, their confidence will become undermined and their judgment brought into question.

However, there are right moments and wrong moments to bid. The "Total Trumps Principle" provides remarkably accurate guidelines as to how high you should be prepared to compete. Later in this section, the suit you choose to bid, the state of the auction, and the position in which you sit are each examined and explained.

Judgment is the key to good bridge, and never more so than in competitive auctions. This section is intended to provide you with the basic knowledge on which to base your decisions. You will find that we return to these basic outlines time and again as we judge when to compete and how aggressive to be.

TOTAL TRUMPS PRINCIPLE

The Value of Trumps

When you hold the clear majority of the points, the number of trumps you hold as a partnership is unlikely to be important. Grand slams with only eight trumps are commonplace. The true value of trumps becomes apparent when the points are fairly evenly divided between the two partnerships, or your side holds the clear minority. In these situations, the combined length of your trump suit is the only factor which should determine to what level you should compete. I really do mean the *only* factor.

The Total Trumps Principle (TTP) underpins all modern aggressive bidding and competitive attitudes, from opening with Weak 2 bids, through barraging the opponents with overcalls and pre-emptive raises, right through to judging whether to sacrifice or double at high levels.

The TTP is tremendously powerful and wonderfully simple. Here it is:

*When the points between the two sides are balanced or your side holds the **minority** of the points, you are safe to compete to the same number of tricks as your side holds cards in your longest suit.*

That is to say, if you believe that you and your partner hold nine spades between you, you will be safe to compete to 3S. It does not mean that you will make it – although you may – it merely indicates that even if you are doubled in this contract you are unlikely to lose more points than if you had left your opponents to play their contract.

This principle assumes equal or favourable vulnerability, so you must be aware of that factor, and it also rests

on both sides playing and defending the contract perfectly which, with the best will in the world, may not always
be possible. However, this is a guiding principle, and it is
very accurate on the vast majority of hands.

Let's take a look at a couple of examples, before
moving on to the precise guidance.

Dealer S
Love All

♠ 43
♡ K109
◇ 962
♣ AK1085

N	E	S	W
–	–	1H	1S
2C	3S	?	

♠ AQJ108
♡ 6532
◇ 84
♣ Q7

♠ K765
♡ 8
◇ QJ107
♣ 6432

W · N · E · S

♠ 92
♡ AQJ74
◇ AK53
♣ J9

West's overcall of 1S is pretty minimum, but totally
sound. Over North's 2C, East jumps to 3S. He knows that
this is a safe manoeuvre because, as his partner holds at
least five spades for his overcall, and as he holds 4-card
support, he knows that there are nine trumps held by his
partnership, and it is therefore safe to jump to the nine
trick level, namely 3S.

Note that he jumps to that level at once. The advantage
of doing this is that it cuts out all the bidding space for the
side with the majority of points. Merely bidding 2S, and
then bidding 3S later is unlikely to be right, as it allows
North and South time to describe their hands further.

Now, what would you bid on South's hand over 3S?
Just about everything is flawed. If you carry right on and

bid 4D, you are a brave man, or woman, and on this occasion you will be rewarded when North corrects to 4H. Others might pass or double, neither of which will be a success.

Notice that 3S fails by only one trick, whereas 4H is a solid Game for North-South. They may reach it anyway, but at least you have made them guess by applying pressure – and applying it safely.

The TTP works particularly well when responding to overcalls, but it can be applied at any time when the points are balanced, or you believe your side holds the minority of points. Indeed, it underpins the entire gamut of pre-emptive bidding. The reason why opening with a Weak 3 is sound is because if you hold seven trumps, you would expect your partner to hold one third of the remaining six trumps, making a total of nine trumps for your side. Hence, you open at the 3-level. The same is true of the very popular Weak 2 opening bids. Here you bid on a very weak hand with a 6-card suit. Once again, you can expect your partner to hold 2-card support, making a total of eight trumps, which means that pre-empting immediately at the two level is both safe and desirable.

Dealer S
E/W Vul.

	♠ 43
	♡ A1032
	◇ Q754
	♣ 1083

N	E	S	W
–	–	3H	Dbl
5H	?		

♠ KJ108		♠ AQ965
♡ 4	N	♡ 6
◇ AK108	W E	◇ J9
♣ KQ97	S	♣ AJ642

	♠ 72
	♡ KQJ9875
	◇ 632
	♣ 5

East should have no difficulty bidding 5S, but will he bid 6S? By bouncing to 5H immediately, North has prevented East-West from using Blackwood, and left them guessing what to do, even though they hold 28 points. As you can see, 6S or 6C are both laydown, but North knew his side held eleven hearts, and could safely barrage to the eleven trick level. If East-West double for penalties instead, they will score +500 – a poor score compared to a vulnerable small slam.

Incidentally, I mention that East-West might double North-South for penalties, but when was the last time you made a penalty double of your opponents looking at a singleton in their suit? That, of course, is the whole point of the TTP. The more trumps you hold, the fewer tricks you will make in defence, and the more likely it is that your opponents will bid on rather than doubling you.

As we will see in the later chapters on "High Level Competitive Bidding", we will be forced into making penalty doubles with singletons and voids in the opponents' suits, just to grab a plus score from the deal. However, most opponents will not know this, and just blunder on in the bidding beyond their safe level.

THE POWER OF SPADES

It is no coincidence that the first example featured a spade overcall and a raise by partner. Being the highest ranking suit, it causes the most obstruction when overcalled, often cutting out a round of bidding for the opponents, forcing them to the next level. For this reason, you should be particularly eager to enter the auction with the spade suit, even if your rules for point-count and suit quality are compromised in the process.

The two purposes of an overcall are to obstruct the opponents' bidding and to attract the correct lead. It is vital to recognize that the first is paramount, and that the second is somewhat overrated as a reason for bidding. Often, your partner is not on lead and, sometimes, even when he is, your overcalled suit is still not right for that particular hand. Of course, your overcall should still indicate an interest in having that suit led but, with spades in particular, it is a very secondary element.

An overcall must always show a 5-card suit. There must never be any compromise on this factor, or your partner will never be able to judge accurately how many trumps you hold between you. However, whereas normally you might expect a suit to be headed by at least two honours – one of them the ace or king – with spades, it is far more important to bid the suit than to worry about suit quality.

Your RHO opens 1D:
On which of the following hands would you overcall 1S?

a)	b)	c)	d)
♠ KQJ86	♠ A10953	♠ Q9642	♠ 86432
♡ 76	♡ A53	♡ A6	♡ AKJ
◇ K532	◇ 7632	◇ K742	◇ 4
♣ Q4	♣ 8	♣ 75	♣ Q1075

Hands a), b), and c) are all worth an overcall of 1S.
They are minimums, but if you do not get involved
in the auction now, you may never get your chance
to bid spades. Of course, overcalling on minimum
point counts, and with poor suits, is risky, but the
relevance of the spade suit is that it offers so much
potential for successful barraging that it is worth the
risk. If your suit was any other than spades, I would
probably pass, feeling that there was too much risk
for too little gain.

d) Despite having a point more than the others, this is
really just too unsuitable for an overcall. With no
values in your long suit and, as we shall see in the
next section, a poor hand make-up, it would be
foolhardy to bid here.

I have made no reference to vulnerability in these
examples, because it is pretty unimportant when considering a 1-level overcall. It is most unlikely that your
opponents will be able to judge correctly whether to
double you for penalties against contracts which they may
be able to make. And, frankly, even if they do possess the
judgment required, they may lack the bidding mechanics
to penalize you anyway.

At the 2-level and higher, vulnerability is very important, because doubling those contracts may offer your
opponents a viable alternative to bidding on in their own
suits.

Overcalling spades should become an obsession for
you because, when part-scores are being competed, the

high ground is 2S. If you can occupy that spot regularly, you will be in a very strong position. With eight spades between you, the TTP is reassuring you that you are in a safe spot, and your opponents will be forced to the 3-level, where you may defeat them. Remember that the number of points you hold between you is utterly irrelevant – you will either be making 2S or failing by an amount equal to, or less costly than, letting your opponents make their contract.

THE CONDITIONS FOR BIDDING

There are several important factors which determine whether it is worth bidding, and how safe it is to compete. These should be considered whenever you are tempted to enter the auction on minimum hands like those in the examples above.

1. How much obstruction will I cause?
The prime purpose of an overcall is to obstruct your opponents' auction, whether merely by your one bid, or because your overcall is the start of a barrage sequence by your partnership. If, however, your overcall does not use up much bidding space then, if it is not supported by your partner, it is more likely to have helped your opponents by pinpointing your distribution and the position of your high cards, than to have had a positive effect for your side. Hence:

> *The more obstructive your overcall, the more aggressive you should be.*
> *The less obstructive your overcall, the more strongly lead directional it should be.*

Your RHO opens 1C:

a) ♠ QJ863	b) ♠ J53	c) ♠ 86
♡ 7	♡ J53	♡ 942
◊ A532	◊ Q9863	◊ KQJ107
♣ J74	♣ A8	♣ A43

a) This is worth an overcall of 1S – just – because by overcalling spades, you have cut out the whole of the

1-level for your opponents. Also, if partner can support you, you have formed the most effective barrage available.

b) This is not worth an overcall of 1D, because this has achieved neither of the objectives of an overcall: it has not used up any bidding space, and it is not necessarily attracting the right lead from your partner.

c) You should overcall 1D here because, although it is not obstructive, it is clear that you want your partner to lead a diamond – it is definitely the best or, at the very least, the safest lead available.

2. How well will the hands fit?

Most players seem very eager to enter the auction with a shortage in the opponent's suit. This is fine when making a take-out double, where your partner will then pick his best suit, and your hand becomes dummy.

Dealer E	♠ 1043	
Game All	♡ Q532	
	◊ 96	
	♣ AK85	

N	E	S	W
–	1H	1S	NB
2S	all pass		

♠ K875	♠ 6
♡ 1095	♡ AKJ87
◊ A84	◊ QJ107
♣ 976	♣ QJ2

```
        N
    W       E
        S
```

♠ AQJ92
♡ 4
◊ K532
♣ 1043

However, when overcalling a 5-card suit, it is often detrimental to your trick taking potential to be short in the opponent's suit, as you may succumb to a forcing defence, having to trump in your own hand, with your side's long trump holding. This is one reason why it is advantageous to hold length in the suit bid on your right. Now, it is more likely that, if your side holds a fit, there will be a shortage in your partner's hand, where you will be able to trump, preserving your own trump length for controlling the hand and drawing trumps.

You may feel that East was a trifle pusillanimous not to compete over 2S, but he is vulnerable and passing out 2S proved a good decision. When West started with ♡10, East-West could lead trumps to prevent a diamond ruff in dummy, and then more hearts to force the declarer. South ended up with four trump tricks and his ♣AK, and that was two down for -200. East-West might make 4H, but it would be tough to reach, and could certainly be defeated with a club ruff.

The point however, was that South's shortage in hearts proved useless to his trick taking potential. Now, we'll swap some cards around:

Dealer E	♠ 1043	N	E	S	W
Game All	♡ 2	–	1H	1S	NB
	◊ Q9632	2S	all pass		
	♣ AK85				

♠ K875		N	♠ 6
♡ Q95	W	E	♡ AKJ87
◊ J84		S	◊ A107
♣ J109			♣ Q732

♠ AQJ92
♡ 10643
◊ K5
♣ 64

Again, East-West might have been more aggressive, but 3H is unlikely to make. Against 2S, notice that South has an easy time making heart ruffs with dummy's small trumps. Even if West finds the excellent lead of a trump, and is then allowed to win the first round of hearts to lead trumps again, South still makes 2S without any difficulty whatsoever.

The other factor of importance is that when you hold length in your RHO's suit, and plan to make ruffs in dummy, there is no danger of being overruffed. If LHO is short in the suit, he will have to play before you decide what to do in dummy.

These same factors are operational when you hold a shortage in your LHO's suit. Again, your partner is likely to be long in the suit and, although you will still be subject to a potential forcing defence, at least you will not be over-ruffed when cross-ruffing.

So, the best conditions for competing are when you hold:

> *length in the suit bid on your right, and*
> *shortage in the suit bid to your left.*

Reverse these shortages, and you and your partner's hands will fit together far less effectively.

3. Offence v Defence

The so-called "offence-defence ratio" analyses how much more useful your hand will be playing the contract, as opposed to defending it. Clearly, the more cards you and your partner hold in one suit, the more important you play the hand with that suit as trumps, rather than trying to defend with it – because, of course, if the opposition are playing the hand, they will be short in your suit, and start trumping in quickly. Take this classic pre-emptive hand:

♠ 8
♡ KQJ10987
◇ 632
♣ 54

This is the perfect pre-empt, because it will score six certain tricks in the play, and quite probably none in defence. Therefore, it is worth the risk of pre-empting to try either to steal the contract, or to push the opposition too high. The difference between the playing strength and the defensive strength is therefore six tricks – a very high number.

♠ Q8
♡ AJ86432
◇ Q106
♣ 5

This hand is far less suitable for a pre-empt, because it contains numerous defensive features. Queens are always useful in defence, and both ♠Q and ◇Q may score a trick. Even the heart suit may produce two tricks in defence. You can probably count this hand as worth at least five tricks in the play, but here the difference is between a playing strength of five, and a defensive potential of three tricks, making a paltry two tricks. What this means is that the hand is almost as good in defence as in the play, so it would be foolish to risk a costly penalty double by pre-empting too aggressively, when the opponents may not be able to make much of a contract themselves.

The playing strength of your hand will always increase if all your values are concentrated in your long suit, and if the "texture" of that suit is good:

a) ♠ KQJ109 b) ♠ AQ1098 c) ♠ AQ532 d) ♠ Q5432

a) Perfect – a rock solid four tricks
b) Very good, four tricks are very likely
c) Same honour cards, but this time you may emerge with no more than two tricks
d) Ghastly – opposite a doubleton in partner's hand, this will be a trump suit from hell.

So, it is the tens, nines and eights which make all the difference. When you hold them, your opponents cannot, and that means that you are far less likely to be subject to a penalty double at low levels.

Whenever you feel that your hand is very good in playing strength, without any defence, you should pre-empt aggressively. When, however, your hand contains points in side suits, or "slow values", such as queens and jacks, you should be more conservative, expecting to take tricks in defence.

Perhaps the best underlying rule of all is that when you are deciding whether to bid on weak hands, do so when all your points are concentrated in the suits you are showing, and not randomly scattered around your hand.

4. Fit and Misfit
The single most important factor in deciding whether to compete, or continue competing, once both opponents have bid, is whether or not they have found a fit. This is because there is a simple rule which applies 99% of the time:

if your opponents have an eight card fit,
your side has an eight card fit

and, conversely,

if your opponents have a misfit,
your side has a misfit

and if the hand is misfitting, you want to be defending.

This can be illustrated by a simple comparison:

W

♠ AK853
♡ 642
◇ 32
♣ K52

N	E	S	W
1H	NB	2C	?

Pass. Your opponents have not found a fit, and both hands are completely unlimited for both strength and distribution. The lead-directional gain of overcalling 2S on this sub-minimum hand is completely outweighed by the danger of a substantial penalty.

This is what I term the "sandwich position" – bidding in between the responder and the opener – and it is the most dangerous position to overcall, with the least to gain: the opposition have already described their hands and, if they believe there is a misfit, they will be in a strong position to opt for penalties rather than wading on into the unknown.

W

♠ AK853
♡ 642
◇ 32
♣ K52

N	E	S	W
1H	NB	2H	?

2S. Your opponents have found a fit – probably, if not definitely, an 8-card fit – and that means that your side also has a fit and it is most likely to be in spades. One of your opponents, South, has also limited his hand, showing weakness and minimum support.

Even if the 2-level is the limit of the hand, and doubling 2S is the correct action for them to take, partnerships who have established a fit are notoriously reluctant to opt for low-level penalties – they usually bid on.

So, be keen to compete, even at the 2 and 3-levels, if your opponents have found a fit, but be cautious of entering the auction, at any level, if no fit has been established, and you suspect a misfit.

PRINCIPLES OF COMPETITIVE BIDDING: KEY FACTS

Total Trumps Principle

- On hands where your side holds the minority of points, or the points are balanced between the partnerships, use the number of trumps held by your partnership to guide you to the correct number of tricks for which you should be contracting.

- Shade your aggressive supporting of partner's over-calls by a trick if vulnerable, if your hand is flat, or your trumps are poor quality.

- Take into account the likely actions of your opponents and the auction to date, and don't pressurise them into doubling you because they have no alternative action.

The Power of Spades
As the highest ranking suit, it is the most pre-emptive.

- Be keen to enter the auction with a spade overcall on sub-minimum hands, particularly at the 1-level.

The Conditions for Bidding
There are seven key factors which will guide you whether to compete and how aggressive you should be:

1. If your opponents have found a fit, then your side holds a fit, and you want to PLAY.

If your opponents have a misfit, then you have a misfit, and you want to DEFEND.

2. You want to compete when:

*   your opponents have found a fit,

*   your opponents have limited their hands.

If both conditions exist, YOU MUST COMPETE.

3. Be reluctant to compete when:

*   your opponents are struggling to find a fit,

*   your opponents have not limited their hands.

If both conditions exist, DO NOT COMPETE.

4. If you compete but your opponents end up playing the hand, you have given them useful information about your hand distribution and the location of points. Compete when:

*   you are causing obstruction, and forming a barrage to use up their bidding space,

*   you want to suggest a sacrifice over your opponents' contract.

5. Your hand is good for competition when your high cards are located in your own long suit(s) or opposite your partner's long suit(s).

Your hand is not useful if your values are located in unbid suits or in the opponent's suit(s). Then, you want to defend.

6. High cards are useful opposite long suits; they are wasted opposite partner's shortages.

If you do hold high cards in partner's short suits, they are only useful if they are aces or king-queens.

Unsupported kings, queens and jacks are all useless opposite shortages in partner's hand.

7. The number of trumps your side holds is the single most important factor when deciding how far to compete.

- Individually, these thoughts are all fairly basic. Yet, taken together they are the principles on which you should judge every close decision each time you need to decide whether or not to compete. When playing against good opponents, you will not get away with reckless competition, but you will benefit hugely from aggressive, sensible interference. If your hands fulfil the requirements outlined in this section, you will succeed in frustrating your opponents, and not your partner.

PART TWO
COMPETITIVE BIDDING

———

To be effective in competition, you and your partner must be certain of the skeleton of the competitive auction – the overcalls. Here, we examine Simple Overcalls, Weak Jump-overcalls, Two-suited Overcalls and Take-out Doubles. The responses to these calls usually present tougher problems than the initial bid – the difference between a barrage and a game-try is enormous, but is frequently confused. This element of the auction becomes simple once both members of the partnership are familiar with the straightforward understandings.

Balancing, or Protective Bidding, occurs not only at the 1-level, but often after several bids. By safely re-opening the auction, you harangue your opposition to a higher level, or steal a contract at a safe level. Your opponents will begin to wonder whether you will ever leave them in peace. And the answer, of course, is no.

Simple gadgets, almost universal amongst experts, such as "Fit-jumps", can be added to your system to provide a huge increase in your competitive accuracy.

The style in this section is pretty aggressive, geared up for duplicate bridge, where low-level competition is at its most fierce. If you blanch at the overt aggression of these methods, strengthen the point-counts a little, even suit quality and length. But, whatever you decide, do it with your partner.

SIMPLE OVERCALLS

This is a short, but very important section.

1. **A simple overcall at the 1-level should always show a 5-card suit.**

   There are times when a 4-card overcall might be right, but if you allow your partnership to indulge in them, the plague of uncertainty will cost you tens of thousands of points more than the rare tactical advantage you may gain. My advice is to agree that every overcall is *always* five cards or more. Besides, it is vital to the Total Trumps Principle that you know, as accurately as possible, how many trumps you hold between you.

2. **The point range for a simple overcall at the 1-level is 7-17 points.**

   It will usually be in the 9-12 points range but, as you will see later, there are times when you should choose a simple overcall on a very strong hand, because every other bid would be even less descriptive than this one.

3. **An overcall at the 1-level is a safe way to compete.** An overcall at the 2-level is dangerous. They are completely different bids.

4. **The requirement for a simple overcall at the 2-level is an opening hand, with a 5 or 6-card suit.**

   You have to be this strong, because now you are offering, even to pairs of modest ability, a relatively simple opportunity to penalize you. Compromise as much as you want at the 1-level, but never at the 2-level,

especially when your LHO has not yet passed, and
particularly when your partner has already passed.

Coming in at the 2-level is dangerous enough, but
entering it when you are in the "sandwich" position
(when there is an opening bid and a change of suit
response) is even more gruesome:

E/W Vul.   **W**

♠ K8
♥ AK853
♦ Q76
♣ 942

N	E	S	W
1S	NB	2C	?

Don't do it! Don't even think about it!

Overcalling 2H here, when you are vulnerable, is mad-
ness. You are not obstructing the opponents' bidding.
You are probably not helping to attract the right lead
because, even if your partner is on lead later, unless he has
a solid attacking club lead, he is likely to lead a heart
anyway. All you are doing by overcalling here is helping
the opposition. They may:

- double you, for some obscenely large penalty, possibly
  involving four digits;

- bid to their normal contract, and now know the distribution and position of the high cards far more accurately than if you had passed;

- bid a game that they would never have found, because
  you have helped them to value their combined holdings correctly.

I don't care for any of these scenarios, especially the first
one, and neither should you.

RESPONDING TO
OVERCALLS

Experts the world over now use very similar methods for responding to overcalls. Certain expert partnerships may have their idiosyncracies, and have developed private arrangements that they have found to work well for them but, fundamentally, they all bid the same way.

Raising Partner's Suit

When your partner overcalls, a raise in partner's suit is based purely on the TTP, and reflects how many trumps are held by the partnership. This raise promises no points, but it does deny interest in game even if partner was strong for his initial overcall.

LHO opens 1H, partner overcalls 1S, RHO bids 2H:

a)	b)	c)	d)
♠ 863	♠ A1095	♠ KQ964	♠ 6432
♡ 7	♡ 53	♡ 6	♡ KJ4
◊ 98532	◊ 7632	◊ QJ742	◊ Q84
♣ KJ42	♣ 653	♣ 75	♣ Q107

a) Raise to 2S. This shows 3-card support for partner's 5-card suit, hence you are bidding at the eight trick level. If partner has overcalled on a minimum, you will not dissuade your opponents from bidding game but, if South is not worth a game bid immediately, you will put their game-try understandings to the test.

b) Raise to 3S. You have nine trumps, so bid at the 9 trick level immediately. This time, your raise may help your partner to find the winning sacrifice.

c) Raise to 4S. Ten trumps, so ten tricks. If your partner
   is not minimum, you may even make this contract. If
   he is weak, the opponents have game on, and must
   decide whether to double or bid on.

d) Raise to 2S. You should shade your response by a
   trick, for although you have nine trumps, your completely flat hand makes bidding to 3S too dangerous.
   Also, you hold no values in spades, but good potential
   for defensive tricks in the opponents' suit, and in the
   side suits.

The more points your partnership hold in your long suit,
the purer the fit, and the more suitable it is to barrage.
Also, the bigger your fit, the fewer tricks you will make in
defence – declarer or dummy will be very short and start
ruffing.

Notice that none of these bids promise any point count.
They are all weak.

Overcaller's Rebid

Generally, the overcaller will pass whatever raise his partner makes, realising that the raise is based solely on trump
length and not points. With a strong hand, partner would
make an Unassuming Cue-bid.

However, as that raise has been made on the assumption
that the overcall was a 5-card suit, if the overcaller holds
a longer suit, he may continue the barrage to the appropriate level.

W		N	E	S	W
♠ 654		–	–	1D	1H
♡ AQJ743					
◇ K6		1S	2H	2S	3H
♣ 32					

Here, West overcalled 1H, and his partner with 3-card support, raised to 2H, knowing that his side held 8 trumps between them. West knew however that they actually held nine trumps, and could therefore bid at the nine trick level.

This rebid by the opener does not show any extra points, only extra length. If the overcaller has a super maximum overcall and wants to try for game, he must introduce a new suit, or bid the opponent's suit.

W		N	E	S	W
♠ 65				1D	1H
♡ AQ743		–	–		
◊ K8		NB	2H	NB	3C
♣ AKJ2					

Over South's 1D opener, West was unsuitable for both double and 1NT, and had to settle for a simple overcall of 1H. When East raises him to 2H, it is a weak bid, based only on 3-card heart support. However, as East's range is probably 0-9 points, it is important that West makes a try for game. By bidding a new suit (or the opponent's suit), West is making a game try, expecting East to rebid 3H if minimum (say 0-6 points), and jump to 4H if maximum.

Although the 3C bid is natural and forcing, as hearts have been agreed as trumps, it would be acceptable to make this bid with a 3-card suit. It is logical however that you should choose a new suit in which you hold some values, so that partner can judge how well his hand is matching with yours.

Showing Support and Strength

Because the range of simple overcalls is very large,

particularly when you are playing Weak Jump Overcalls, it is important to be able to question the overcaller as to their strength, to examine the possibilities of game.

At the 1-level, a simple overcall may be as weak as 7 points or as strong as 17 points; at the 2-level, the range is 10-17 points. So, in response, there will be many hands where you will wish to be in game if partner is close to maximum for his overcall, whereas a part-score will be quite sufficient if he is towards the minimum end of his range.

As responder to the overcall, whenever you hold 3-card support or better and a well-shaped 10 points or more (closer to a 1NT opener with a flat hand) opposite a 1-level overcall, or any 10 point hand opposite a 2-level overcall – hands which will make game opposite an over-call at the maximum end of the range, you should always begin proceedings with an Unassuming Cue-bid. This convoluted sounding bid is, in fact, merely a bid of the opener's (your opponent's) suit at the lowest available level.

This asks your partner a simple question: are you min-imum or maximum for your overcall?

If he is minimum, he will rebid his suit at the lowest available level, and you will then pass or make a further try for game.

If he is maximum, he will describe his hand further, in one of the following ways:

- with a 6-card suit, he will jump a level in his suit

- with another 4-card suit, he will show this suit

- with a stopper in the opponent's suit, he bids NTs.

- with none of the above, but a strong hand, he will think of something other than merely re-bidding his suit at the lowest available level.

South opens 1C; North and South then pass:

1. W

W	E
♠ AK853	♠ Q74
♡ Q63	♡ KJ5
◇ 743	◇ J85
♣ 42	♣ AQ65

W	E
1S	2C
2S	pass

West has overcalled on a minimum hand so, when East makes an Unassuming Cue-bid, showing 3-card spade support and an interest in game, West makes the weakest bid possible, by rebidding his suit at the lowest available level.

2. W

W	E
♠ AQJ98	♠ K63
♡ A4	♡ KJ53
◇ QJ76	◇ AK52
♣ 85	♣ 63

W	E
1S	2C
2D	4S

Over East's Unassuming Cue-bid, West shows his other suit. Any bid, other than a rebid of the original overcalled suit at the lowest available level, shows that the overcall was not made on a minimum hand. East bids game confidently because of the known double fit.

3. W

W	E
♠ AK853	♠ Q74
♡ 863	♡ AQ5
◇ 743	◇ AJ85
♣ AQ	♣ J85

W	E
1S	2C
2NT	3NT

West's 2NT rebid promises one certain stopper in the opener's suit. Here, despite the 8-card spade fit, 4S may prove tricky, whereas 3NT should present few problems.

4. W	E	W	E
♠ AQJ986	♠ K53	1S	2C
♡ A4	♡ KJ53		
◊ 762	◊ AK95	3S	4S
♣ 85	♣ 63		

West shows his non-minimum hand, by jumping in his overcalled suit, to show a 6-card spade suit.

Although the Unassuming Cue-bid suggests 3-card support, if you have a very good hand with only doubleton support you may still decide to use an Unassuming Cue-bid to discover more about your partner's hand before trying for or bidding game.

It is vital to distinguish between a raise in the over-caller's suit, which is always weak, and the UCB which shows values, and confirms that your side definitely holds the majority of points.

Changing Suit After an Overcall

This is another situation where different players adopt different styles. I recommend a change of suit should be played as non-forcing, showing a good quality 5-card suit or longer, and is certainly lead-directional.

The meaning changes slightly, but significantly, depending upon whether there is an intervening bid by the opener's partner before you have your say. If the opener's partner passes, it is more likely that your partner has a strong hand and, if you should pass, your partner's overcall may get passed out. You will therefore be more keen to introduce your suit, even without tolerance for your partner's suit. When the opener's partner makes a response, it is less likely that your partner's overcall is strong, and you should avoid joining the auction unless you have a fit with partner's overcalled suit.

1. *South opens 1C; North passes:*

W	E
♠ AK853	♠ 4
♡ Q63	♡ AJ985
◇ A43	◇ KQ87
♣ 42	♣ 965

W	E
1S	2H
3H	pass

When North passes over West's 1S overcall, it suggests that West may be quite strong so, despite the misfit in spades, East is worth a bid of 2H to show his reasonable quality heart suit. Although any change of suit is completely non-forcing, it always shows a 5-card suit, so West is worth the raise. If East had been even a tiny bit stronger, he would have bid on to game.

2. *South opens 1C; North responds 2D*

W	E
♠ AQJ98	♠ 3
♡ 4	♡ KQ952
◇ J762	◇ A53
♣ 853	♣ Q642

W	E
1S	pass

North's response of 2D marks West with a minimum overcall (opener has, say, 13 points, East holds 11 points, North holds at least 8 points – this leaves 8 points for West). With no fit for West's spades, East should not enter the auction. Notice that no one has an 8-card fit on this deal – indeed, the only 7-card fits available to North-South are in hearts and spades! They will definitely struggle in whatever contract they eventually reach. Sit back and enjoy!

Responding NTs
Many players forget that an overcall may be very much weaker than an opening bid, and respond NTs in the same way to both bids.

A 1-level overcall may be as weak as 7 points, so it makes sense that NT responses should be much stronger than usual.

In order to bid 1NT, you should believe that your side holds about 20-22 points, assuming that your partner holds the average type of overcall of, say, 9 points. Opposite a 1-level overcall, therefore, a 1NT response should show about 10-12 points, and include tolerance for a major suit, or even support for a minor suit. It guarantees two stoppers in the opponent's suit.

A 2NT response will show 13-15 points opposite a 1-level overcall, and 11-13 points opposite a 2-level overcall.

If your partner is known to be more aggressive than usual for his overcalls, you will increase your requirements for the NT response. If he errs on the side of conservatism, you can afford to slacken your own requirements.

Fit-jumps in Response to Overcalls
These are becoming increasingly popular as the level of

aggression and competitiveness continues to develop. When there are long suits around, players often find themselves having to make crucial bidding decisions at very high levels. These are tough at the best of times, but the pressure is certainly eased if you have a good picture of your partner's hand.

N/S Vul. W

♠ 8
♡ AK853
◇ KQ3
♣ 9842

N	E	S	W
–	–	1S	2H
2S	4H	4S	?

What are you going to do? Pass, double, or bid 5H? At this favourable vulnerability, it is a tough decision. Although your side may hold ten hearts between you – hence, partner's leap to 4H – you may still hold enough defensive tricks to beat 4S. Perhaps, you will score a heart, two diamonds, and partner will provide a trump trick? It would be disastrous to sacrifice when North-South were not making their contract, as 5H surely stands no chance whatsoever. If only we knew more about partner's hand....

N/S Vul. W

♠ 8
♡ AK853
◇ KQ3
♣ 9842

N	E	S	W
–	–	1S	2H
2S	4D	4S	?

This time, partner has jumped, not to 4H, but to 4D. This is a fit-jump, showing support for your hearts, plus a 5-card suit or longer, headed by some top honours.

Now, it is easy for you to bid 5H, or even 5D, because you know that you hold a double fit, and that all your values are concentrated in those suits. That makes your defensive prospects decidedly poor, and the offensive strength of your hand much greater.

As a general rule, it will be wrong to compete to the 5-level without at least ten trumps in your suit. However, when you hold a double fit with partner, you can compete to the higher levels with confidence.

Let's take a look at the entire deal (you and your partner are now North-South):

Dealer E
E/W Vul.

	♠ 943		
	♡ Q964		
	♢ AJ1096		
	♣ 5		

N	E	S	W
–	1S	2H	2S
4D	4S	5H	NB
NB	Dbl	all pass	

♠ J752		♠ AKQ106
♡ J107	**N**	♡ 2
♢ 82	**W E**	♢ 754
♣ KJ76	**S**	♣ AQ105

	♠ 8		
	♡ AK853		
	♢ KQ3		
	♣ 9842		

This is what happens when there are double fits around. 5H makes! The important element of the deal is that had North merely bid 3H or even jumped to 4H, South would never have been able to make an informed decision about whether he should bid on, double or pass. In fact, if North does merely support hearts, South should never bid on to 5H, and East-West will make their game, instead of North-South scoring their doubled contract.

This hand was a little unusual, in that both sides can make so many tricks. However, this occurs because there is what is known as a "double, double fit", which means that both sides have a fit in two suits. When you know that you hold a double fit with partner, you are nearly always safe to compete further than you might think, as the tricks tend to pour in.

A fit-jump occurs whenever you jump one level in your own suit after partner's overcall.

- You should make a fit-jump whenever you have good support for your partner's overcall, plus a 5-card suit or longer, headed by at least ace or king.

- Your point count will vary from quite weak – you are minimum in the example above – to quite strong hands, generally short of an opening hand.

- In terms of support for partner's suit, the recommendation is that you have at least 3-card support. At higher levels, you should hold the right number of trumps according to the TTP – so that when your partner returns to his suit, he is at an appropriate level. However, you can shade this by one, if your own suit is good quality.

- Fit-jumps occur below game level. Any jump in a new
  suit at the game level is natural and to play, and does
  not promise support for partner's suit.

So, in the example above, North held 4-card support for
South's hearts, making a total of nine trumps. However,
he was safe to bid at the 4-level because he held his decent
second suit.

WEAK JUMP OVERCALLS

These overcalls fit in perfectly with the TTP, and are based on similar principles to the Weak 2 Opening bids, described in Part 3 "Strengthening Your System".

Whilst Medium or Intermediate strength overcalls are still the norm for rubber bridge players, duplicate players cannot afford to have bids in their armoury which occur relatively infrequently. The Weak Jump Overcall tends to occur far more often, because the point range is lower and, as we all know, we are far more likely to pick up bad hands than good ones!

Hand Requirements

As with all jump overcalls, whatever their agreed strength, these bids promise 6-card suits of good quality. However, quality is largely in the mind of the beholder and, when you are dealing with hands with as few as 6 points, it is tough to hope for the top three honours...

The only purpose of these overcalls is to be obstructive; they are only very mildly lead-directional. As you hold a 6-card suit, and you can reasonably expect partner to hold 2-card support, so you have an 8-card fit, and wish to be at the 2-level as quickly as possible.

For a bid at the 2-level, your point range should be about 5-9 points; for an overcall at the 3-level, maybe 6-10 points. The main factors, however, are good suit quality and texture (the tens, nines and eights), and good conditions for bidding.

Love All. RHO opens 1C:

a)	b)	c)	d)
♠ KQJ987	♠ 84	♠ 4	♠ Q76432
♡ 76	♡ 53	♡ KJ10987	♡ KJ4
◇ 98	◇ QJ10987	◇ 82	◇ A84
♣ 842	♣ K53	♣ 7543	♣ 3

a) 2S. A perfect Weak Jump Overcall, in the same way that it is a text-book Weak 2 opener. The Offence-Defence ratio strongly suggests a pre-empt: the hand will make five tricks if spades are trumps, one at most if in defence.

b) 2D. Another very good hand for a Weak Jump Overcall. The opponents almost certainly have a fit in one of the majors, and your bid will make it tougher for them to find it and to judge the correct level. Notice the excellent texture of the diamond suit.

c) 2H. An absolute minimum, but the length in the RHO's suit, and the solid texture of the hearts make it well worthwhile to interfere.

d) 1S. The spade suit is disgusting, you are short in your RHO's suit, which lessens the chance of a good fit with partner, and you have excellent defensive potential in hearts and diamonds. It is simply not worth the risks of a Weak Jump Overcall when you may well be beating your opponents' game contract with very little help from partner. Content yourself with a 1S overcall, and if partner supports you, you can decide whether to bid on to show your 6-card suit.

Game All. RHO opens 1S:

a)	b)	c)	d)
♠ 9873	♠ 82	♠ 4	♠ 6432
♡ 7	♡ 4	♡ KJ10987	♡ KJ4
◊ KQJ1098	◊ 642	◊ 82	◊ AQ5432
♣ 42	♣ QJ98764	♣ 7543	♣ –

a) 3D. Fine. You may be vulnerable, and this may go for a number, but the odds are good that partner will be very short in spades, and therefore may well hold 3-card diamond support. If that is so, 3D will play nicely. Importantly, you have no defensive potential, so it is worth the risks involved.

b) 3C. Despite the 7-card suit, you are nowhere near worth a vulnerable pre-empt to 4C. 3C causes trouble for the opponents and keeps you at a relatively safe level.

c) Pass. Definitely Pass. This is a mile short when vulnerable. In fact, it's several miles short, because you shouldn't even consider 3H when not vulnerable. You have too little to gain, and too much to lose.

d) Pass. Despite length in spades, why do you want to bid? If the opponents reach 4H or 4S, do you really want your partner to sacrifice in 5D? Certainly not. Partner has clubs, and that is only of interest to you if you are defending. Even 2D is risky; it is unlikely to gain much, and the threat of a big double if diamonds are stacked should keep you quiet.

When you hold a hand where you would have made an
Intermediate Jump Overcall, you must make a simple
overcall first and then, providing the auction has not
accelerated too quickly, rebid your suit on the next round
of bidding.

			N	E	S	W
W			—	—	1D	1H
♠ J6			1S	NB	2D	2H
♡ AKQ853						
◇ 93						
♣ A42						

Your rebid of hearts shows a 6-card suit and confirms that
you hold the type of hand that would have made an old-
fashioned Intermediate Jump Overcall.

RESPONDING TO A WEAK JUMP OVERCALL

The purpose of the Weak Jump Overcall was to disrupt the auction. Only if you hold a very strong hand, or a distributional hand with support, should you consider bidding. If you have an opening hand with a doubleton in partner's suit, just remember that partner may have a 6-count. Then pass... If the opposition bid on, you will be well placed; if they don't, your partner may, just may, struggle home in his contract.

Weak Hands with Support

The Total Trumps Principle is in operation again, but make sure that you really need to continue the barrage before wading in. Often, partner's WJO has done the damage, and there is no need for you to try to put icing on the cake:

Love All. Your LHO opened 1H, partner overcalled 2S, RHO passed:

a) ♠ 986   b) ♠ KQ6   c) ♠ AQ84
    ♡ 732   ♡ 5   ♡ 8
    ◊ KJ82   ◊ A876   ◊ 9832
    ♣ KQ2   ♣ 87653   ♣ 7543

a) Pass. Yes, you have nine spades between you, but your hand has some defensive potential, and your opponents may not have a fit. As they rate to hold the majority of the points, if you bid 3S and the opener makes a take-out double, this may get passed out for penalties. This would be fine if your opponents could make something, but can they? Partner's 2S has given them a tough decision. Let them get on with it.

b) 3S. This time your points are mostly in your long suit, you have some shape, and the opponents have a heart fit. They can probably make 4H, but you may put the opener off from bidding again if you barrage immediately.

c) 4S. You have ten spades, so bid ten tricks straight away. All your values are in spades, so the opposition have a certain game, even a slam. Don't expect to play there, the opener will almost certainly bid again, but at least he, and later his partner, will have some tough decisions to make.

Fit-jumps

These can be played in just the same way as over simple overcalls, to help partner judge whether or not to sacrifice. You will want to ensure that all your values – however meagre – are concentrated in your support for partner and in your own suit:

Love All. Your LHO opened 1H, partner overcalled 2S, RHO bids 3C:

a) ♠ KJ6   b) ♠ Q986
   ♡ 72   ♡ 5
   ◊ AKJ82   ◊ KQJ876
   ♣ 982   ♣ 83

a) 4D. The jump into your new suit promises 3-card support or better for partner's spades, and shows a good quality 5-card diamond suit. When your opponents bid 4H, if your partner has a fit with you in diamonds, he may choose to sacrifice, and with a shortage in diamonds, he will know to pass, and lead that suit.

b) 4D. This time when the opponents bid 4H, you will bid 4S if your partner doesn't (you have ten trumps after all). Then, if the opponents bid to 5H, your partner can judge whether to bid again (unlikely, but possible) or pass.

The fit-jump will operate with or without the intervening opponent making a positive bid.

Strong Hands

This is the time you wish you were not playing Weak Jump Overcalls, because it is your bidding that has been disrupted and not your opponents'.

The most important rule is, do not get over-excited. Your partner has a very weak hand, so you must be very strong to bid on. Different partnerships have different arrangements, but I think it is best to streamline your system so that bids mean the same things in similar situations. Hence, as with responses to a Weak 2 opening, any change of suit is non-forcing (probably to play there), 2NT and 3NT are very strong, again to play.

An Unassuming Cue-bid, when there is room, is a game try, showing at least 2-card support, and a very strong hand. Otherwise, the obstructive nature of the Weak Jump Overcall will affect you as much as you hoped it would affect your opponents, and you will be forced to guess what to do.

Love All. Your LHO opened 1H, partner overcalled 2S, RHO passed:

a)	b)	c)	d)
♠ A6	♠ AQ8	♠ 7	♠ KJ4
♡ A32	♡ AQ5	♡ AJ42	♡ 98
◊ KJ82	◊ Q87	◊ A432	◊ AQ832
♣ Q542	♣ K983	♣ AK83	♣ AQ3

a) Pass. Even if your partner has a 9-count, which is his absolute maximum, game may still be a mile away. Think of it another way. If you had opened 1NT, and partner had made a weak take-out to 2S, would you bid on? (If you would, please close this book now, it could cause you untold harm...)

b) 2NT. If partner has a 6-count, this is enough; if he is maximum, you expect him to raise you, or bid 4S. Notice, that you hold a fit with partner. Without a fit do not bid NTs, just pass.

c) Pass. If partner has a hand which makes game a good bet, he was too strong for a Weak Jump Overcall. You have four tricks; maybe he has four tricks. That makes 2S a pretty promising contract. If you pass quietly, and the opposition re-enter the fray, you will soon cheer up.

d) 3H. The Unassuming Cue-bid, showing strength and support, and trying for game. If partner is maximum, say, ♠AQ7532, and ♣K, you will want to be in game, and he will bid it (if he is minimum, he will rebid 3S, and you should pass). But, your hand is not as good as it looks, as most of the outstanding strength is sitting over it in your LHO's opening hand.

MICHAELS CUE-BIDS AND UNUSUAL NO-TRUMP OVERCALLS

These two gadgets showing 2-suited hands are considered pretty standard these days, and you should be familiar with them. As you should never make a take-out double at the 1-level with a 2-suited hand, it is important to be able to show such hands with these or similar gadgets. As you will see, they are very closely related bids, which is why we will deal with the strategy behind them simultaneously.

First, let's clarify what each of these bids mean and how to make them. Then, we will discuss when and why to make them, which is far more important.

Michaels Cue-bids
Michaels cue-bids can be made either directly over the opening bid, or in the protective position.

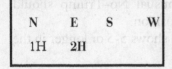

N	E	S	W
1H	2H		

or

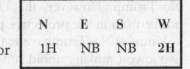

N	E	S	W
1H	NB	NB	2H

If the opponent opens a minor suit, a Michaels cue-bid shows both major suits; if the opponent opens a major suit, the cue-bid shows the other major suit and one of the minor suits.

Opponent opens	You bid	Showing
1C	2C	5-5 or longer in the majors
1D	2D	5-5 or longer in the majors
1H	2H	5-5 or longer in spades, and one of the minors
1S	2S	5-5 or longer in hearts, and one of the minors

- Suit quality and texture must be very good.

- The hand should contain 10 points or more. There is no upper limit.

Responses – in brief – to Michaels Cue-bids
If the intervening opponent passes, you are forced to show preference between partner's two suits. With strong hands with good support, give jump-preference.

If partner has cue-bid a major suit, and you wish to find out which of the two minor suits he holds, you respond 2NT, asking him to name his minor suit.

Unusual No-Trump Overcall
Any overcall of NTs which is not natural is the Unusual No-Trump. However, the Unusual No-Trump should not be used in the protective position.

Unusual No-Trump overcall shows 5-5 or longer in the two lowest ranking unbid suits.

Note: It is illegal not to specify at least one suit with a 2-suited overcall. Hence, it is not permitted to state that the Unusual No-Trump shows any two of three unbid suits.

Opponent opens	You bid	Showing
1C	2NT	5-5 or longer in diamonds and hearts
1D	2NT	5-5 or longer in clubs and hearts
1H	2NT	5-5 or longer in the minors
1S	2NT	5-5 or longer in the minors

- Suit quality and texture must be very good.

- The hand should contain 10 points or more. There is no upper limit.

Responses – in brief – to Unusual No-trump Overcalls

If the intervening opponent passes, you are forced to show preference between partner's two suits. With strong hands with good support, give jump-preference.

MAKING TWO-SUITED OVERCALLS

Whenever one has special gadgets, it is very hard to resist the temptation to wheel them out at the least possible excuse, and show them off to everyone. However, it is absolutely vital that we do not use these conventions indiscriminately.

The purpose of these gadgets is to obstruct the opponents' auction, and to suggest a possible sacrifice. However, you must realise that, if you end up defending the hand, you will have given the declarer a massive amount of distributional and, to some extent, point-count information on which to base his plans.

Indeed, your opponents are far more likely to make their contract if you have intervened with a Michaels or Unusual No-trump than if you had passed throughout.

Hand Make-up
Having decided that you will enter the auction, there is only one consideration:

- Suit quality.

You do not want to risk an overcall which will result in a 2 or 3-level contract, without a high-quality trump suit, particularly as partner may have a poor fit with you. Remember that the better your trumps, the poorer your opponents' trumps, and therefore the less likely they will be to opt to double you in close situations.

As 10 points is recommended as a minimum, you may not be able to hold that many honours in each suit, but the texture must be good. Keep reminding yourself that the more points you hold in your long suits, the better it is to play; the more points in your short suits, the better it is to defend.

In short, you want all your points in your two suits.

Love All. Your RHO opened 1S:

a)	b)	c)	d)
♠ 6	♠ 82	♠ K	♠ 4
♡ KQJ98	♡ 5	♡ AJ	♡ KQ98
◇ KQJ98	◇ QJ1098	◇ KJ432	◇ AQJ832
♣ 42	♣ KQJ98	♣ Q8543	♣ 32

a) 2S. Perfect. This is your textbook example. It's a pity it will never come up at the table, but then examples in textbooks almost never do.

b) 2NT. Only 9 points, but your suits are exquisite. Look at that texture!

c) Pass. Resist the temptation. Your hand is packed with defence – more than half your points are in hearts and spades. If your LHO has the remainder of the points, your 3-level minor suit contract will be a disaster.

d) 2D. Not a Michaels. I include it because some people seem to think that "5-5 in two suits" means 10 cards any old place. It doesn't.

Love All.

e)
♠ 6
♡ 8
◇ AQJ86
♣ AKJ985

N	E	S	W
–	–	1S	2NT
NB	3D	NB	?

e) Remembering that partner may have nothing – not
    even three diamonds as you have made him bid –
    what should you bid now?

    4C. This shows a very strong hand, and must be a
    game-try, showing extra length in clubs. Partner could
    hold anything from a Yarborough with a doubleton
    diamond (or worse!) to, maybe, 9 points with four
    little diamonds.

    If he is minimum, he will pass or rebid 4D, and will
    face a struggle. With something approaching a maxi-
    mum, he will bid to game. With everything in
    between, he will look only at aces in the outside suits
    (he will know you only hold two cards in hearts and
    spades) and the points he holds in your known suits,
    then he will make the best decision possible.

Responses to Michaels Cue-bid or Unusual No-trump
When your partner makes a Michaels or an Unusual
No-trump, if the next opponent passes, you have to show
preference. If you are strong with a fit, you should jump
in your preferred suit, or go to game.

*Love All. Your LHO opened 1H, partner overcalled 2H
(Michaels showing spades and a minor suit), RHO
passed:*

a)	b)	c)	d)
♠ J62	♠ 8	♠ AJ76	♠ 4
♡ 98632	♡ 8754	♡ 8732	♡ KJ98
◇ AJ82	◇ K872	◇ AQ2	◇ AQ83
♣ 2	♣ K983	♣ A3	♣ AQ32

a) 2S. Partner is likely to hold spades and clubs, so settle
    for a relatively safe 2S.

b) 2NT. This asks partner to name his minor suit. Whichever it is, you will pass, and it will be better than playing in spades.

c) 4S. You have a good fit in spades, and an excellent secondary fit in whichever minor suit partner holds. As he is promising a minimum 10 points, you have the right point count too.

d) 3NT. A little awkward, but you have a known fit in a minor suit, and your values in hearts will be waste-paper if you play in 5C or 5D. In 3NT, they are excellent stoppers, and partner has the spades covered. There may be a little struggle for the ninth trick, but at least you know where all the outstanding points lie. Whatever your LHO leads, he will help you.

General Guidelines

• If your RHO bids, you can pass if weak or without a fit for partner, or bid on if you want to compete.

• If your RHO doubles – which will be for penalties – bid only if you have clear preference for one of partner's suits rather than the other. Bidding will not show any points, merely length preference, just like bidding over a redouble.

Considering the Sacrifice

Obviously vulnerability will come into your decision, as well as the form of the game. Rubber bridge and teams of four players will be far less keen to sacrifice than duplicate pairs players. The latter group have a clear target at which to aim, making decisions easier.

Generally, you will only want to compete to the 5-level
with a 10-card fit in your long suit, or with a double fit (an
8-card fit in two suits). Without this, you do not have
sufficient trump strength to warrant the risks of a
sacrifice.

In keeping with the rules for the original overcall, you
will want your values concentrated in your partner's suits,
not in the opponents' where they may be useful in
defence.

In short, the more length you hold in your partner's
suits, and the more points in those long suits, the keener
you should be to sacrifice.

***Not Vulnerable, against Vulnerable opponents. Your LHO
opens 1H, partner overcalls 2NT, RHO bids 4H:***

a)	b)	c)	d)
♠ AQJ6	♠ 8732	♠ KJ75	♠ 9542
♡ 932	♡ 52	♡ Q108	♡ 5
◊ KJ8	◊ 7	◊ A432	◊ KQ83
♣ 432	♣ A98632	♣ 83	♣ A983

a) Pass. You do have a double fit with partner, but the
   majority of your points are in a suit in which your
   opponents hold length. The worst result is if you go
   two off doubled for -300, when the opponents were
   not making their contract. There is too great a risk of
   the "phantom sacrifice" on this deal.

b) 5C. You have no defence to their contract, and eleven
   clubs between you. If they bid 5H, pass, and hope for
   a diamond ruff.

c) Pass. You only hold nine diamonds between you, and
   you want ten trumps to be at the 5-level. Those major

suit values will be completely worthless to you in 5C, but offer plenty of defensive potential against 4H.

d) 4NT. Not Blackwood, but asking partner to pick his trump suit. You are expecting ten tricks in the minor suits in 5C or 5D, and you are very unlikely to take more than three tricks in defence.

I do not want to encourage you to sacrifice too freely, because it is not a winning strategy. However, if you and your partner have understood the principles behind making these two suited overcalls, you will see that it is easier to judge what to do when you know that partner's suits are of good quality, however weak or strong he may be.

Keep in mind the need for at least ten trumps, or a double fit, to bid at the 5-level, and also the refrain:

> *the more length you hold in your partner's suits,
> and the more points in those long suits, the keener
> you should be to sacrifice.*

1NT OVERCALL

I like 16-18 points as my range, but whatever you and your partner agree is just fine.

Now, test yourself on the next set of hands and, more importantly, test your partner:

Love All. RHO opens 1D:

a)	b)	c)	d)
♠ AQ6	♠ K97	♠ Q8	♠ 92
♡ A32	♡ Q8652	♡ Q108	♡ 985
◇ K432	◇ AQ9	◇ AJ10	◇ K3
♣ J32	♣ AQ	♣ KQJ83	♣ AKQJ98

a) Pass. Whatever your agreed range, this is a clear-cut pass. It is a very nasty 14 points, with only one stop in diamonds, and not a decent intermediate in sight. The important element of this hand is that you realise it is a pass fairly quickly. If you sit staring at it for hours, if your LHO passes, your partner will not be able to protect without a very good hand. Get used to recognizing this as rubbish and passing smoothly. Do not even contemplate a take-out double. It is essential to have a shortage of your opponent's suit for this action, and you don't, so you can't.

b) 1NT. This is partnership style. It seems logical to emphasize shape and point count rather than the 5-card heart suit. If partner has four hearts and uses Stayman, then I'll be happy to have them as trumps. See whether your partner agrees that a 1NT overcall could contain a poor quality (or even high quality) 5-card major suit.

c) 1NT. 15 points, plus another for the 5-card suit, and some more for the tens. This is worth at least 17 points in NTs.

d) 1NT. I would make this bid at rubber, teams or duplicate pairs. On the expected diamond lead, you will make seven tricks. If you are doubled, you can run to 2C. If partner raises you to game, his points will be in the majors.

Do not fret about the single diamond stopper. You only need one stop when you will not have to lose the lead to establish your source of tricks.

1NT is the high ground when the points are divided equally between the two partnerships and there are no long suits. You have a huge advantage if you are the first to bid 1NT. It may make, it may go one off – either way, you have a good result. If your opponents want to bid on, they do so at the 2-level, and your partner can judge whether to bid on, pass, or double.

But, and it is a big but, you must have either a source of tricks, or excellent stuffing (tens, nines, and eights) which will make it hard for the defence to make a breakthrough in more than one suit.

That is why hands c) and d) above are so much better than a flat 16-count. Try to think of a 1NT overcall less as showing a balanced hand, and more as a simple desire to hog the last 1-level contract, and play the hand in the denomination which scores the most for the least tricks.

NOTE: if you play Stayman, transfers, or anything else, opposite a 1NT opener, you should agree to play the same gadgets opposite the 1NT overcall.

TAKE-OUT DOUBLES

Double is, by far, the most flexible of the competitive manoeuvres, involving partner in the decision fully. When we examine how to survive the barrage we will see how its use is vital during competitive part-scores, and also for involving partner in high level decisions.

In this section, we will examine the different uses of a take-out double, when used after a 1-level opening bid by your opponents.

Standard Take-out Doubles

The standard take-out double includes two vital elements, which should never be compromised.

1. **A shortage in the opponent's suit.** This means two cards or fewer. If you make a take-out double with more cards than this, partner will never be able to judge the distributional strength of your hand effectively.

W

♠ AJ7532
♡ 642
◇ A95
♣ 4

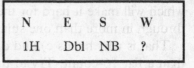

N	E	S	W
1H	Dbl	NB	?

Your response on this hand should be 4S. You can make this bid, because you know that you hold an excellent fit, with the distribution working completely in your favour. The weakest element of your hand, the three small hearts,

64

is opposite a known shortage in partner's hand. If you were not certain that partner was short in hearts, you would be forced to bid more modestly, and then the whole principle of responding to a take-out double is compromised.

The basis of this principle is that you always bid as many of your best suit as you think you can make, assuming partner holds a 13-count 4-4-4-1 hand. If you respond on that basis, you will always hit a sensible spot.

2. **3-card support, or better, for every unbid suit.** This means that you will never make a take-out double at low levels on a 2-suited hand. Over pre-empts, this does not apply, as you have lost too much bidding space to be able to retain perfect accuracy.

W
- ♠ KJ432
- ♡ AQ2
- ◇ K9
- ♣ 432

N	E	S	W
1C	Dbl	NB	?

Your response should be 4S. If, however, there was any chance of partner not holding at least 3-card support, you would be forced to turn somersaults before reaching the best contract when, in fact, this is an obvious bid.

Overcall or Double?
Should you make a take-out double, or overcall 1S?

RHO opens 1D:

♠ AQ987
♡ KQ2
◇ 5
♣ K984

The advantage of double is that it will get across your general shape and point-count. The disadvantage is that you may miss your 5-3 fit and end in an uncomfortable 4-3 fit.

Generally then, it is better to overcall your 5-card major on hands where you are 5-3 in the major suits, planning to double subsequently for take-out if the opponents continue to compete in diamonds. For instance:

W

♠ AQ987
♡ KQ2
◇ 5
♣ K984

N	E	S	W
–	–	1D	1S
2D	NB	NB	**Dbl**

Now, you have got across that you have a take-out double hand, including a 5-card major suit. In fact, your partner's failure to support your spade overcall means that he does not hold 3-card spade support, so you can be confident that either a heart or club contract will be superior.

Note that this sequence is completely different from:

N	E	S	W
–	–	1D	Dbl
2D	NB	NB	2S

This shows a very strong 1-suited hand, unsuitable for an initial overcall.

When you are 5-4 in the major suits, double becomes the superior option. You will almost certainly play in your longest trump fit because, if partner has equal length in the majors, he will cue-bid the opponents' suit to discover which you prefer.

Double with Very Strong Hands
What action would you take on each of these hands?

Love All. RHO opens 1D:

a) ♠ AQ6   b) ♠ AKQ987
   ♡ A106   ♡ K2
   ◇ KQ2   ◇ A93
   ♣ AQ92   ♣ 65

a) You are too strong to overcall 1NT, and 2NT would be Unusual No-Trump. Double and follow up with a NT rebid over partner's response. Assuming that your 1NT overcall range is 16-18 points, double, followed by a NT rebid at the lowest available level, shows 19-21 points, with two stops in the opponent's suit.

b) On single-suited hands of 7 playing tricks or more, with a 6-card suit (or superb quality 5-card suit), double initially and, over partner's response, show your suit.

If your hand is worth 8 playing tricks, you can double and then bid at the 2-level immediately. With 9 playing tricks, at the 3-level, etc.

These are the only types of hand when you are permitted to double without a shortage in the opponent's suit. However, here, double is merely a prelude to your rebid, revealing a very strong hand.

Take-out Doubles After Two Suits Have Been Bid

A double here shows at least 4-4 in the two remaining suits, but you should not bid indiscriminately. If you have little chance of buying the contract, you will give away important information to the opponent who ends up as declarer. Also, it will be easier for the opponents to catch you in a penalty double if the suits are behaving badly, because they will have discovered their own misfit by the time you have entered the auction. For this reason, it is sensible to ensure that the double shows a good point-count, or better, 5-4 in your two suits.

With 5-5 distribution or better, you would opt for an Unusual No-trump rather than a take-out double.

W
♠ 543
♡ AK63
◊ 4
♣ AQ952

N	E	S	W
1D	NB	1S	Dbl

Double is much better than merely overcalling 2C, as it brings the heart suit into the picture. Notice that you do not need to hold shortage in both of the opponents' suits, but that you should hold your high card values in the suits you are showing.

Having passed, it is wise to restrict take-out doubles in this position to hands containing 5-4 distribution in the unbid suits.

Responses to Take-out Doubles

You should assume that your partner is 4-4-4-1 with a 13-count and bid as many of your best suit as you think your side can make.

If you have alternative places to play, you should begin proceedings with an Unassuming Cue-bid.

W
- ♠ AQ54
- ♡ KJ63
- ◇ 943
- ♣ K5

N	E	S	W
1D	Dbl	NB	2D

You want to be in game, but you are not sure whether to play in hearts or spades – the doubler may have four cards in one and only three in the other. Clearly, if you held four hearts and four clubs, you would opt to play in the major suit, so this Unassuming Cue-bid asks the doubler to choose between his major suits.

Most experts play that an Unassuming Cue-bid shows at least 11 points. In addition to this, you can play that an Unassuming Cue-bid can be made with 8-10 points only when it guarantees four cards in both major suits. The Unassuming Cue-bid is designed to get you to your 8-card fit, regardless of whether you plan to play in game, or just short of it.

The Unassuming Cue-bid can be used at any level.

W
- ♠ AQ54
- ♡ KJ63
- ◇ 94
- ♣ K52

N	E	S	W
1D	Dbl	3D	4D

Again, 4D asks the doubler to choose between the major suits.

Doubler's Rebid

When you make a take-out double and your partner makes a jump response, how excited should you become?

W
♠ AK87
♡ QJ63
◇ 9
♣ K985

N	E	S	W
–	–	1D	Dbl
NB	2S	NB	?

Pass. When you doubled, you showed partner your diamond shortage, your opening hand values, and your support for spades. Partner has assumed that you are 4-4-4-1 with a 13-count, and he has chosen to bid 2S. As you have nothing extra for your bid, you should not even consider bidding on.

Unless you are considerably stronger than the standard take-out double, you will always pass your partner's limit response.

W
♠ AK87
♡ AJ63
◇ 9
♣ KQ85

N	E	S	W
–	–	1D	Dbl
NB	1S	NB	?

2S. Any rebid by the doubler shows a very strong hand, with extra points and 4-card support for the responder's suit.

Your rebid of 2S shows extra values above those shown by your initial take-out double, and invites partner to bid game if he was absolutely maximum for his initial response.

BALANCING

Balancing, or protective bidding, is one of the elements of the game which distinguishes the serious player from the social player, because it involves an understanding of the complete deal, rather than just the thirteen cards in your sticky little hand. Once you understand what balancing is about, you will realise why it is wrong to compete with balanced hands, but right to enter the fray with weak distributional hands.

It is almost always wrong to let the opponents play at the 1-level or at the 2-level if they have found a fit quickly. However, these are quite different situations, and we will examine them separately.

A Bid and Two Passes
This is the position which most people think about when they hear the term "protection".

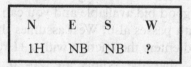

N	E	S	W
1H	NB	NB	?

You should almost always bid here because if the points are equally divided between the two partnerships – and it is very likely that they are – it must be right either to steal the contract or to push your opponents to an unsafe level.

You can be reassured by the Total Trumps Principle that as you must have a 7-card fit somewhere, the 1-level will always be right and, as you may well hold an 8-card fit, the 2-level will be safe.

There are many rules you can remember for bidding in this position (including the "theory of the transferred

king", with which you may be familiar) but by far the eas-
iest is this:

> *After a bid and two passes, everyone at the table*
> *should assume that the points are divided 20-20*
> *between the two partnerships.*

Your opponents could have 25 points, and your side
might have even more but, for the vast majority of the
time, you will find that the 20-20 assumption is pretty
accurate. In this way, when you compete with a very weak
hand, your partner will not get overexcited.

♠ 973	N	♠ AQ54				
♡ AQJ96	W E	♡ K3	N	E	S	W
◇ 85	S	◇ K94	1D	NB	NB	1H
♣ 863		♣ J952	NB	1NT	all pass	

This demonstrates how smoothly a balancing sequence
runs.

Over North's 1D, East has no good bid to make so he
passes – this is the essence of good partnership bridge: if
you have no good bid available and you can pass, do.

When South passes also, West assumes that the points
are 20-20 and enters the auction with a 1H overcall. East
also assumes that the points are 20-20, but in case
partner has a reasonable hand, he makes one small show
of strength. His 1NT response shows a strong hand
(probably 11-13 points), and invites West to bid on if he
was stronger than expected for his overcall. West is not, so
passes, and 1NT becomes the excellent final contract.
East will certainly make seven tricks and, with South
marked with 0-5 points, the spade finesse will probably
produce an overtrick. That all adds up to a very good
result at duplicate pairs.

In short then, bids that you make in the balancing

position will represent the same distributional characteristics of bidding in the direct position, but may lack the points, assuming that partner will deal with that half of the equation.

General Guidelines for Balancing

Simple Overcall should always be a 5-card suit, but with a wider range of about 6-14 points.

Double will show shortage in the opponent's suit and a choice of the remaining suits. Although there is no upper limit for the bid, a minimum hand may be as weak as 8 points. You will also double with hands that are too strong for a 1NT overcall, but not strong enough for a 2NT overcall (see below).

1NT overcall will show a balanced hand with one stopper or better in the opponent's suit. Range to be agreed by partnership, but commonly 11-14 points.

Stayman, transfers, and whatever else you may play in response to a direct overcall of 1NT should be played here also.

With all these bids being made on weak hands, it is important to have a couple of bids which definitely show strong hands. These are:

Jump Overcall Whatever your usual style, these are always played as strong in the balancing position, showing a 6-card suit, with solid opening hand values.

2NT overcall This should never be played as the Unusual No-trump in the balancing position, but instead to show a strong balanced hand with at least one stopper in the opponent's suit and 19-21 points.

Double, followed by a NT rebid   On balanced hands of 15-18 points, which fall between the range for an overcall of 1NT or 2NT, the correct procedure is to double initially and, over partner's response, rebid No-trump at the lowest available level. This may take you beyond a safe level, but it is not easy to describe this type of hand safely, and this is the best of some bad alternatives.

LHO opens 1H, then two passes to you. What will you bid on these hands?

a)	b)	c)	d)
♠ AQ6	♠ K973	♠ Q82	♠ A92
♡ A72	♡ 2	♡ J42	♡ A85
◇ J852	◇ QJ94	◇ AQ10	◇ K3
♣ J96	♣ K983	♣ KQ32	♣ AKQ98

a)   1NT. A bit spartan, but it will usually gain to bid on these hands rather than pass. One stopper in hearts is adequate for a protective 1NT.

b)   Double. Perfect shape, and partner will be aware that you could be this weak when he responds.

c)   1NT. I know that ♡Jxx is not a stopper, but the choice is between this, pass, and double. Double must show a shortage in the opponent's suit at all times, and pass seems far too submissive for these modern times. This is why most experts do not expect a stopper every time they hear their partner overcall 1NT in the balancing position.

d) 2NT. Perfect point-count, hopefully five club tricks.

Your partner is most likely to hold a strong hand and be unable to compete when he holds length in the opponent's suit. Therefore, when you are short in that suit you can be more confident of a strong balanced hand opposite you.

If you are long in the opponent's suit, it is more likely your partner is short, so you must ask yourself why he failed to compete initially at his turn.

Finally, you should consider not protecting if you believe the opponents may have a far superior trump suit to the one they are currently declaring. Again, your clue may come from inferences drawn from your partner's silence.

LHO opens 1H, then two passes to you. What will you bid on these hands?

a) ♠ 6   b) ♠ AQ73
   ♡ J972   ♡ KJ985
   ◊ AQ852   ◊ 94
   ♣ Q96   ♣ 83

a) Pass. It would be quite reasonable to make a balancing overcall of 2D, but for the matter of spades. If your partner has the 11 points which we expect him to hold, he clearly does not hold a 5-card spade suit, or he would have overcalled 1S. Whilst you may be able to make some number of diamonds, maybe even some NTs, there is a very real danger that if you bid, your opponents will discover their spade fit – they definitely hold eight between them, if not more – and outbid you in the part-score battle or even, conceivably, reach game in spades.

b) Pass. Your defensive prospects against 1H are quite
   reasonable, and there is a danger that your opponents
   may hold a minor suit fit, which they may find if you
   allow the opener to bid again. Your partner is,
   presumably, short in hearts, yet he has failed to bid, so
   he is not strong, and he does not hold a robust 5 or
   6-card minor suit.

Throughout the gamut of balancing bids and sequences,
there is the constant risk of, on the one hand getting to too
high a level and, on the other possibly missing game.
Protective bidding is not amongst the most accurate in the
game, but it remains a vital battleground at the part-score,
and one into which any successful partnership must throw
themselves with gusto, if they wish to prevail at club or
tournament level.

Balancing at Higher Levels

The balancing position occurs at any level when there has
been a bid or bids, followed by two passes. Much of the
time, the opponents will bid to their contract, and you will
merely pass it out and begin to defend.

However, when the auction ends at a low level, it may
well be right for your side to become involved in the
auction, either to steal the contract – whether or not it
makes – or to push the opponents higher.

If the opponents fail to agree a trump suit quickly, you
do not want to enter the auction. A misfit is good for only
one thing – defending – and your opponents will relish the
opportunity to defend against your contract rather than
struggling on in their own.

If, on the other hand, your opponents find a fit quickly, then you are in a much stronger position to join the
bidding. The simple facts of bridge life are that if your
opponents have a misfit, then you are likely to have one

also, whereas if they have a fit, your side is likely to have one too.

> *Indeed, if your opponents hold an 8-card fit, it is virtually certain that your side also holds an 8-card fit.*

Remembering our Total Trumps Principle, this means that we are safe to compete to the 2-level, however few points we hold between us. Often it is right to compete to the 3-level with only eight trumps. Bidding on, providing we have a fit, has so much to gain and comparatively little to lose. We may make our contract. We may go down by one, or even two tricks, and this will still be a better score than allowing the opponents to make their 2-level contract. The biggest upside of all however – yet one which is overlooked by many players – is that your opponents may choose to bid on to the 3-level themselves. Once they do that, you cannot lose. Either they make their contract, and you have lost nothing, or they fail, and you convert a minus score into a plus score.

In these situations, when you find yourself in the balancing position, you will find that both opponents have limited their hands. For this reason, you can once again assume that the points are divided 20-20 between the two partnerships.

Your aim is to steal a contract at the 2-level and, sometimes, at the 3-level, or push the opponents to the 3-level, where you will leave them to play and, hopefully, fail.

You have overcalls, doubles, and the Unusual NT at your disposal, and each will be based not on point-count, but merely on suitable shape.

You are West:

a) ♠ J6432   b) ♠ 97   c) ♠ Q987
   ♡ 2   ♡ 52   ♡ 5
   ◊ A32   ◊ KQJ9   ◊ AJ103
   ♣ K932   ♣ QJ987   ♣ Q964

N	E	S	W
–	–	1H	NB
2H	NB	NB	?

a) 2S. You correctly refrained from overcalling 1S initially, but now there is a very good chance of your side holding an 8-card spade fit, and no chance of your partner becoming overexcited.

b) 2NT. This is the Unusual No-trump. Although your partner would normally expect 5-5 distribution, in the balancing position he should be aware that you are quite likely to be only 5-4. This is superior to double, because you have no spade support.

c) Double. You are hoping to hear 2S from partner, but 3C or 3D should not distress you. All being well, the opponents will press on to 3H, and your partner's heart holding will come into its own.

It is vital to remember that the points are likely to be 20-20, so that when your partner balances, you do not punish him by overbidding:

You are West:

a) ♠ KQ6   b) ♠ 97   c) ♠ QJ98
   ♡ 975   ♡ AQ97   ♡ 8532
   ◊ AJ2   ◊ AQ9   ◊ AQJ3
   ♣ K932   ♣ J987   ♣ 4

N	E	S	W
1H	NB	2H	NB
NB	2S	3H	?

a) Pass. Don't even think of bidding on. You have achieved your aim, which was to nudge your opponents out of a safe 2H into a potentially unsafe 3H.

Also, your partner balanced because he expected you to have this hand. The whole point of balancing is that the more points you have, the fewer your partner holds. On the basis that the points are 20-20, he has 7 points.

b) Pass. Don't give a penalty double so much as a second's thought. Your partner has a pile of old rubbish and possibly, just possibly, he has pushed your opponents too high. If they go down, you have a great result. If they make it, you have an average result. If you double and they make, it is a catastrophe, and it's all your fault.

c) 3S. OK, it was time to give you a break. You have nine spades, your partner has a singleton or void heart and you a singleton club. This time, you are bidding 3S to make, even if partner is Ace to five spades and nothing else. Please notice that, as well as a nicely distributed hand, you also have 4-card support, making a minimum of nine trumps for your side.

If the opponents open a suit, make a simple raise, and then pass, it is virtually mandatory to bid. They have both limited their hands, and they have found a fit. Everything is right for you. This is particularly true of weaker players who will take exception to you butting in with your protective bid, and they will almost always bid on. I have had opponents groan at me and say, "Don't you ever let us play a hand quietly?" Smile disarmingly, and try to resist saying out loud, "Not if I can help it."

The moment you develop a reputation amongst your friends or club members for being tough to play against, you have gained a huge psychological advantage, and it will pay dividends each and every time you sit down to play against them.

Balancing after 1NT

Most people play a weak NT at duplicate pairs these days. Even in countries like France and the USA, which are still hotbeds of strong NT play amongst rubber and Chicago players, a weaker NT is being played at duplicate by a growing number of people.

Hopefully, you already realise why it is so sensible. If the points are balanced, there is a huge advantage to be the first person to bid 1NT, and an even bigger advantage to being allowed to play in 1NT. Make or fail, it is usually a good result.

For this reason, it is important to interfere over 1NT as often as possible, especially when you are weak and distributional. Let me give you an example:

Non-Vul. against Vul. opponents,
Your RHO opens 1NT (12-14):

a)   ♠   AQ982   b)   ♠   QJ10987
       ♡   K82   ♡   52
       ◊   A32   ◊   KQJ9
       ♣   32   ♣   7

a) Most players would bid 2S over 1NT on this hand, but it will often prove wrong. If your LHO holds the remaining points, you may get doubled and go for a big score. If your partner has points, he may find it hard to know what to bid.

   The fact is that you should be quite happy to defend against 1NT with this hand, because you have a good quality long suit to lead, and enough outside entries with which to regain the lead and cash your winners. Put it another way: if you make eight tricks in 2S, you score +110; if you make the same eight tricks against 1NT, you score +200. At Pairs, that is a huge score; even at rubber or Chicago, it is a significant gain.

b) Many players would like to bid 2S, but would be afraid that partner would count them for a stronger hand. Here, however, your hand is very unlikely to be useful in defence because, even if you establish your spade suit, you may not regain the lead to enjoy the winners. Playing in 2S though looks just dandy, with your well-textured spades and nice diamonds.

The fact is that if your side holds the majority of points and a long suit, you may score better by defending 1NT, especially if the opponents are vulnerable. Whereas, if your side holds the minority of points with a long suit, you will do better to play at the 2-level.

How you bid over 1NT, and whether you elect to use conventional gadgets to assist you, is a matter of partnership choice. However, I strongly recommend that you adopt an aggressive balancing attitude to bidding over 1NT so that you can steal extra contracts from your opponents.

To this end, you should agree that all bids in fourth seat after a 1NT opening are based solely on distribution, including any conventional defence to 1NT you may play.

LHO opens 1NT, then two passes to you:

a)	b)	c)	d)
♠ KJ8643	♠ A32	♠ A4	♠ QJ2
♡ 92	♡ 5	♡ Q1087	♡ A5
◇ K8	◇ AQJ76	◇ 32	◇ AKQ83
♣ 432	♣ 8632	♣ QJ987	♣ 983

a) 2S. Your partner is quite likely to have 2-card support, giving you an 8-card fit, so 2S is as safe as houses. You should bid in this position with any 6-card suit, regardless of point-count (assuming a minimum of, say, 6 points) or suit quality.

b) 2D. Only a 5-card suit, but good quality. If you had been on lead, you might have been happy to defend against 1NT and lead a diamond but as your partner wouldn't have led a diamond your defensive potential is greatly reduced, so cause some trouble instead. If you are playing with a partner who would have led a diamond anyway, you are a lucky pony, and you probably don't need my help...

c) 2C – if you are playing natural overcalls. If you are playing a conventional defence to 1NT, use it now to show your two suits.

d) Double. Because a double of 1NT is always for penalties, the point-count should not be compromised very much. Whatever partner leads should still leave you in with a good chance of a decent plus score.

> *The same attitude should also be adopted when the partner of the 1NT opener has already passed.*

In both cases, although no fit has been established, both players have limited their hands, and so entering the auction is safe.

The only danger of this policy is that, very rarely, you may miss game. However, this is a tiny loss compared to the huge advantages to be gained from disrupting your opponents' 1NT contract far more frequently.

You should also make the same bids on each hand in another situation. If your RHO opens 1NT third-in-hand – his partner has already passed – you are instantly in the balancing position, because both hands have limited their strength. But make sure your partner realises this.

There is a real danger that you will miss a game contract on rare occasions. Each time that you bid on a weak distributional hand, you are hoping that your partner passed with a flat hand and the balance of the 20 points which you have assumed to be held between the two partnerships. When he holds that hand, he will pass.

The one time he might consider bidding on is when he holds a very strong hand, say 13-15 points, with 4-card support for a major suit and some reasonable distribution.

Now, he should decide to raise you and, if you are not minimum, you may reach game. **The fact is that, unless your side holds *all* the remaining points, you are very unlikely to make game after a 1NT opening by the opposition, unless you hold nine trumps between you.**

At other times, when you note that game could have been made, just reflect on all the bids you were able to make which your opponents could not because they were playing a much more restrictive system. After all, the main reason for playing the weak NT is that it is so tough to compete against – that's why *you* are playing it.

Balancing After a Weak Take-out

This is exactly the same as the 1NT balancing position, in that you do not need to wait for the 1NT opener to pass, because he has already limited his hand. So either you or your partner can bid in the balancing style after a weak take-out.

Indeed, the weak take-out bidder has positively screamed that it is right for you to bid. After all, he is announcing that he is weak, and that he is frightened to play in NT because of a pronounced shortage in at least one suit. So you must pounce. Get to thinking: whichever suit is weak, I want it as our trumps.

LHO opens 1NT, partner passes, RHO bids 2H (weak take-out):

a)	b)	c)	d)
♠ K8643	♠ A732	♠ 9	♠ 92
♡ 54	♡ 5	♡ 87	♡ KJ987
◊ 754	◊ QJ82	◊ KJ962	◊ AK83
♣ KQ4	♣ J1095	♣ QJ987	♣ A3

a) 2S. Straight in there with your 5-card suit, never mind the quality. 2S is where we want to play if that is our 8-card fit and if we don't bid them, we can't expect to get there. Assuming the points are 20-20, partner has a nice, flat 12-count waiting for us.

b) Double, for take-out. Hopefully partner will bid 2S, but 3C or 3D won't be a disaster.

c) 2NT. Unusual. You have the shape, partner has the points. Tell him that you don't want to hear about his raggedy spade suit, but want him to pick a minor.

d) Pass. As double is for take-out, you must pass here, and hope that partner can dredge up a bid, and that his choice is double. If it is, you will convert it to penalties by passing. If he bids 2S, you won't even think of bidding 2NT, you will just pass. If he has the sort of hand you had in a), 2S will be quite high enough.

This is, as you can see, aggressive stuff, and from time to time you will come unstuck. However, whatever form of the game you play, you only need to be right 60% of the time and you're going to be a big winner. This bidding will be right even more often than that. But be warned, don't try this with new partners, and be prepared to display large quantities of humility and good humour for the times your aggression costs you a fat penalty. Belief that this is a winning attitude will see you through the tough times.

THIRD-IN-HAND OPENERS

Clearly, as these are opening bids, they are not strictly competitive bids. However, if there are two passes to you, and you hold a weak, distributional hand, you can be pretty certain that the fourth player is going to bid. You are just going to get your competition in before he even starts.

All good players know that third-in-hand openers can be a little weaker than usual, and we are not really concerned with that here. However, there are some tactical points it is worth mentioning.

The Short Pre-empt

Many players pre-empt with 6-card suits in all positions. I am a pretty strong advocate of keeping pre-empts up to strength and length before partner has had a chance to bid so that, if he happens to hold the strong hand, he will have some idea what to do.

Once partner has passed, however, you can be much freer in your approach, and third-in-hand is the place to be aggressive:

Non Vul. against Vul. Two passes to you:

a) ♠ KQJ1098   b) ♠ Q987652   c) ♠ 4
    ♡ 92   ♡ 532   ♡ 8
    ◊ 8643   ◊ AQ   ◊ QJ9876
    ♣ 4   ♣ 2   ♣ A9754

a) 3S. Notice the excellent suit quality, and the complete lack of defence for any other contract. Well worth the risk.

b) 3S. I hope that you would not open with a pre-empt ahead of your partner with this garbage. However, third in hand, there can be no pressure on partner, just on the opponents.

c) 3D. You might pass and come in with an Unusual No-trump, but with partner having passed, it looks like they have game on, and I want to make them work.

Alternative Openers

Two passes to you:

a)	♠ 82	b)	♠ KQJ2
	♡ 92		♡ 532
	◇ AKQJ87		◇ A43
	♣ J75		♣ K85

a) All sorts of possibilities, but the worst is 1D. This may be an accurate description of your hand, but it is causing no obstruction to your LHO. 3D would be quite in order – there is no problem being too strong for a pre-empt third in hand, as you won't be missing game, and all your partner can possibly do is support you.

Personally, I quite fancy 1NT. It's mildly pre-emptive, it'll be a fine contract if you end up there, and, above all, it will cause an opposing declarer to misplace the outstanding cards when he comes to play the contract. If 1NT is doubled, you might pass and try for a fabulous score, or you might take the sensible way out and bid 2D.

b) 1S. Of course this is a 1NT opener, but a Weak NT third in hand is quite risky, particularly vulnerable, and 1S is just as pre-emptive. It also has the advantage of attracting the best lead from partner. If partner responds, you are going to have to pass, which won't be too bad. Hopefully, partner will either support you, or just pass, and leave the opponents to get on with it.

Non Vul. against Vul. Two passes to you:

  c) ♠ KQJ109
       ♡ 972
       ◇ 8643
       ♣ 4

c) 3S. That is what many top tournament players would bid at duplicate pairs. They reckon that the quality of the spades will protect you from a penalty double, and that you will cause sufficient obstruction to warrant the risk. Notice the favourable vulnerability. Personally, I think it's just a bit frisky even by my standards. If you play Weak 2s, this is perfect for a third in hand Weak 2S at any vulnerability, and that would be my choice.

The advantage of pre-empting third in hand is that your passed partner cannot possibly bid anything other than to support you.

> *Generally, if you open third in hand with a pre-empt of any kind at the 2-level (if you are playing Weak 2s), the 3-level or higher, your partner should assume that you hold one fewer card than usual for your bid. In this way, he will not overestimate by how much he should continue the barrage when he applies the Total Trumps Principle.*

Light Openers

Many players like opening the bidding on ten or eleven points in all positions, especially third-in-hand. In my view, without a 6-card suit, this is a losing tactic in the long run.

Considering how aggressive our system is already, to open light on 5-card suited hands is a step too far. Keep opening bids, even third-in-hand, up to full strength or containing a 6-card suit or longer.

Hand (c), above, should be reserved for rare occasions only.

COMPETITIVE BIDDING: KEY FACTS

Simple Overcalls and Responses

Simple overcalls

Our system is based exclusively on 5-card overcalls, or longer.

Raising partner's overcall

- Supporting partner's overcall is always weak.
- Whether you make a simple raise or jump raises, you are guaranteeing no points whatsoever; just trump length based on the Total Trumps Principle.

Overcaller's rebid

- The original overcaller continues the barrage only with extra trumps, not because he is stronger. Bidding on in the same suit never shows strength, just more cards in the suit.
- If the overcaller is super-maximum, he makes a game try by bidding a new suit or the opponents' suit.

Showing support and strength

- On hands with 3-card support or more, where there is a chance of game opposite a maximum overcall, you must make an Unassuming Cue-bid. Opposite a 1-level overcall, this will generally show at least 10 points, usually more. The overcaller then defines his hand further. If minimum, he rebids his suit at the lowest available level; if stronger, he will show his additional features.

Changing the suit after an overcall

- A change of suit is non-forcing, and shows a high-quality 5-card suit or longer.

- If the bid is made without intervention from the preceding opponent, no support, or even tolerance, for partner's suit is required. If the preceding opponent bids, you should only enter the auction if your suit is extremely good, or if you hold tolerance or weak support for your partner's suit.

Responding NTs

- NT responses are much stronger than opposite opening bids, and promise two stoppers in the opponent's suit, and suggest at least 2-card support for the over-called suit.

- In response to a 1-level overcall:
  1NT shows 10-12 points; 2NT shows 13-15 points.
  In response to a 2-level overcall:
  2NT shows 11-13 points; 3NT shows a good 13 points+

Fit jumps in response to overcalls

- A fit jump is a weak bid, showing additional shape to a normal barrage raise.

- Jumping in a new suit shows at least 3-card support for partner's suit, and a 5-card suit or longer, headed by at least two honours, including ace or king.

Weak Jump Overcalls and Responses

- Always a 6-card suit, or longer.

- Obstructive and not lead-directional. Suit quality is paramount.

- In response, be wary of aggressive support, even non-vulnerable – the original jump overcall has often reaped adequate chaos.

2-Suited Overcalls

For Unusual No-Trump and Michaels Cue-bids 5-5 is the minimum distribution.

- Suit quality, with good intermediates, is essential.

- Values must be concentrated in your long suits, not scattered around the hand.

Only make a 2-suited overcall when you both want to buy the contract (as a sacrifice if necessary) and when you believe that you will buy it because, if your opponents end up as declarer, your descriptive overcall may help them to make their contract.

1NT Overcall

This can be made, not only on a balanced hand of 16-18 points, but also on hands with a long, usually minor, suit.

- You require two stoppers in the opponent's suit when overcalling 1NT on a flat balanced hand, but only one stopper if your hand contains a solid source of quick tricks.

Take-Out Doubles

Double on non-standard hands when you hold:

- flat hands of 19 points+. Rebid NT over partner's response.

- 7 playing trick hands with a 6-card suit; rebid your suit over partner's response.

Emphasise 5-card major suits, preferring to overcall this suit rather than doubling. A subsequent take-out double can be made to introduce the remaining suits.

Responding to take-out doubles

- Assume the doubler is 4-4-4-1 with 13 points and bid as many of your best suit as you can make.

- With more than one possible trump suit, use an Unassuming Cue-bid (generally showing 11 points+) to obtain further information from the doubler.

On standard 4-4-4-1 type take-out double hands, the doubler will pass all partner's responses unless he is extra strong, or responder makes an Unassuming Cue-bid.

Balancing

Aim to steal a low-level contract or push your opponents to an unsafe level.

- If you push your opponents from the 2-level to the 3-level, leave them there. Do not continue bidding, and risk a penalty.

- In the balancing position, do not use the Unusual NT or Weak Jump overcalls. In the fourth position: 2NT shows a flat 19-21 points;
  Jump overcalls are strong: high-quality 6-card suit and opening hand values.

- Be extra keen to compete when one or both opponents have limited their hands: after 1NT and weak take-out and, especially, after weak suit agreement and two passes.

Third-in-hand Openers

Aim to be destructive with these opening bids.

- Be wary of opening a Weak NT third-in-hand when vulnerable. Bid your best quality 4-card suit instead, and pass partner's response.

- When responding to a third-in-hand Weak 2 or pre-emptive 3-opener, assume partner holds one card fewer than usual for his bid – then support according to the Total Trumps Principle.

PART THREE
STRENGTHENING YOUR SYSTEM

I N this part, we will examine various conventions and partnership understandings which can strengthen your system, and make your bidding more accurate and harder to play against. I play all these gadgets, and highly recommend them. However, there are many slight variations to the content of the conventions, and you will find that different players favour one rather than the other. I think that my suggestions are simple to remember, logical, and, for the most part, as accurate as you would wish. Before playing any of these gadgets, do check that your partner plays them in the same manner.

There are those who believe that conventions and systems are playing too strong a role in bridge these days. I would agree with them, particularly when conventions are invented solely to confuse the opposition about the strength and make-up of the hand. With gadgets like Weak 2s, however, everyone at the table knows that they show a weak hand with a long suit so, although they cause great disruption, they are natural bids, which everyone can understand. That seems to be absolutely within the spirit of the game.

For The Macallan International Pairs Championship, for which I am the administrator, I was charged by the players to legislate on a more natural and straightforward set of systems and conventions allowed for the tournament. Out went Strong Clubs, like Precision and the Blue Club, out went the Multi 2D, and all the calls which don't clarify whether the hand is weak or strong or what suits might be held. All the gadgets described in this section are permitted, and all them were played by almost every pair. If the vast majority of the best players in the world play them, then I think we can be confident that we should do so too. Each of the elements is self-sufficient and you can choose to add one, or any combination of them, to your system.

WEAK 2 OPENERS

We had better get used to Weak 2s: opening them, responding to them, competing over them because, soon, the whole world will be playing them.

Of all the gadgets which you might add to your system, this is one that I would include first. There are many forms of Weak 2s available – this is a simple form, which leaves most of the Acol system unaltered, whilst optimizing the aggressive pre-emptive approach required for success. As you will see, all the bids and responses conform perfectly with the Total Trumps Principle described in the first section.

Weak 2H and 2S Openers

2H and 2S are weak, pre-emptive opening bids, showing a 6-card suit, and 5-9 points. Third in hand, the range is likely to be much wider, and fourth in hand, you are likely to be rather stronger than usual.

When vulnerable, your suit quality should be extra good; non-vulnerable openers, especially in spades, may compromise on suit quality.

With your 6-card suit, you can expect your partner to hold 2-card support, giving you an 8-card fit, which makes a 2-level contract completely safe however few points you may hold between you.

Like all pre-emptive manoeuvres, the quality and texture of your suit is all important. Ideally, all your points will be concentrated in your long suit, and you should not have more than one defensive trick outside your suit. In this way, your partner can better judge what to bid in competitive auctions.

Personally, I am not a fan of a Weak 2D opener, since it is less pre-emptive and leaves Acol players with only 2C as a strong opener. This spoils an excellent part of the system.

You are the dealer:

a)	b)	c)	d)
♠ KQJ1098	♠ 97	♠ Q4	♠ 92
♡ 86	♡ KQ9865	♡ Q65432	♡ AQJ985
◇ 432	◇ K94	◇ AJ93	◇ A3
♣ 92	♣ 32	♣ 7	♣ 984

a) 2S. The absolutely ideal Weak 2 opener, with excellent trumps, and no defensive values whatsoever.

b) 2H. Good suit quality, with just a little something outside.

c) Pass. Suit quality is too poor, and you have too many values outside your long suit. These will be more useful in defence than when playing the hand.

d) 1H. You are too strong for a Weak 2. 1H, followed by a 2H rebid, will describe this hand perfectly.

Hands c) and d) can be considered borderline 2H openers third in hand, when partner has already passed, and there is only your LHO to upset. When there is a chance that your partner could hold a strong hand, it would be unwise to compromise the requirements for the bid.

Responding to 2H and 2S
There are many different conventional responses available, and many different agreements as to what is forcing or not. Here, we will look at a version that is simple to learn and remember, and surprisingly powerful.

- All raises in your suit are weak and based on the TTP.
- Any change of suit is weak and to play.
- Opener will always pass both these responses.

Partner opens 2S, RHO passes:

a)	b)	c)	d)
♠ AQ6	♠ K973	♠ 8	♠ 92
♡ 32	♡ 2	♡ 1085	♡ Q985
◇ J10432	◇ A952	◇ AQJ1097	◇ K3
♣ 932	♣ 8632	♣ K63	♣ AQJ98

a) 3S. You have nine spades between you, with your values concentrated in your long suit. This makes your hands strong to play in spades, but weak in defence. Your opponents almost certainly have game on, and you must make it hard for them to find it.

b) 4S. Now, you have ten trumps, so you will not make more than one defensive trick in spades, your ◇A, and partner's possible one defensive trick outside of spades. So, 4H is cold for the opposition, and bidding 4S is a convincing method of preventing them from bidding it.

c) 3D. This seems likely to play better than 2S. Partner will pass.

d) Pass. You have an 8-card fit in spades, so it would be foolish to bid 3C. If partner is maximum, he should make 2S; if he is minimum, he will fail by a trick or two, but the opponents will have part-score available to them.

The crafty thing about Weak 2s is that you will raise 2H to 4H and 2S to 4S on two very different types of hand.

You may be very weak and distributional with 4 or 5-card support, merely barraging the opposition out of the action, or you may be strong with good support, and you are bidding the game contract you expect to make. It doesn't matter a jot that your partner can't distinguish between these two situations, as he will have to pass whatever your bid means. But it will certainly unsettle your opponents. They won't know whether you have bid a normal game, or whether you have swindled them out of a hand where they have game or even a slam available. The 4-level is awfully high to enter the auction, just to find out . . .

Forcing 2NT Response

If you have a strong hand, where you feel game may be on, the positive response to a Weak 2 opener is 2NT. This is the one forcing response, and asks the opener to describe his hand further. Before making this response, it is important to remind yourself that your partner is very weak and that he was hoping to disrupt the opposition's bidding and not his own partnership. Therefore, you will have to have a very good hand to commit your side to at least the 3-level. With 2-card support, you will need at least 16 points; with 3-card support, maybe 14 or 15 points; with 4-card support, any well-shaped opening hand. These point-counts are indications only; distribution is all.

Following your 2NT response, the opener's rebids are as follows:

- With a minimum hand, he always rebids his suit at the 3-level.

- With a maximum hand, he has three alternatives:

1) With a strong suit, headed by two of the top three honours, he rebids 3NT, offering responder a chance to pass, bid 4H or 4S, or look for a slam.

2) With a more broken suit, the opener rebids a suit in which he holds his outside values. This will help the responder to judge which contract will play best.

3) With a trump suit that will play well opposite a small doubleton, but missing two of the top three honours, jump to 4H or 4S immediately.

Rebidding After the 2NT Response
Particularly at duplicate bridge, it is important to keep open the option to play in 3NT, as well as game in the opener's major suit. The first two responses keep this option open, whereas the third response bypasses 3NT, as it is now very unlikely to be the right contract.

You open 2H, partner responds 2NT. What should you rebid?

a)	b)	c)	d)
♠ 63	♠ 97	♠ Q8	♠ 92
♡ KQ10987	♡ AJ9876	♡ AQJ1087	♡ QJ10987
◇ 85	◇ KJ8	◇ 765	◇ 3
♣ 932	♣ 43	♣ 83	♣ AJ98

a) 3H. You are a minimum opener.

b) 3D. You are a maximum opener, with decent suit quality, but lacking two of the top three honours. Showing you have some outside values in diamonds will allow responder to make an informed choice of final contract.

c) 3NT. You have two of the top three honours in hearts, and a maximum opener. Partner can pass with ♡Kx and stoppers in the other suits, or bid onto game or slam in hearts.

d) 4H. If your partner held ♡AK, he should have bid 3NT himself. On that basis, your distributional hand is unsuitable for NTs, and your solid trumps will play well, even opposite a small doubleton in partner's hand.

Although these responses are quite straightforward, they will help your partner to judge what to do next.

Partner opens 2H, you respond 2NT, partner rebids 3C:

a)	b)	c)	d)
♠ AQ6	♠ 97	♠ QJ32	♠ 2
♡ KQ2	♡ K82	♡ AQ8	♡ AQ85
◊ A8432	◊ AJ3	◊ AQ85	◊ A65
♣ 32	♣ AQ987	♣ 52	♣ AQJ98

Opener is maximum, with an outside value in clubs.

a) 3NT. You can count six heart tricks, and two aces. Partner has a stopper in clubs. If you don't get the expected spade lead – which gives you your ninth trick immediately – the worst scenario is having to rely on the spade finesse.

b) 4H. It seems likely your partner holds ♣K, so the club fit makes ten tricks seem eminently achievable.

c) 3H. You have made your game-try on a fairly minimum hand, and your partner's news that he holds something in clubs does not particularly please you. If he had held a value in spades or diamonds, you might have been tempted to have a go at 4H.

d) 6H. Partner's club value must be ♣K, so you can count twelve tricks (six hearts, five clubs, and ♢A) assuming partner has not opened 2H on a jack-high suit. Certainly, he should never do this, other than, perhaps, third in hand.

Partner opens 2H, you respond 2NT, partner rebids 3NT:

a) ♠ QJ6   b) ♠ 7
   ♡ Q2   ♡ K82
   ♢ Q932   ♢ KQ43
   ♣ AKQ2   ♣ AQ987

Opener is maximum, with two of the top three honours in hearts.

a) Pass. As partner has ♡AKxxxx, you should make six heart tricks and three club tricks and, providing the defence cannot cash five tricks in spades and diamonds first, make 3NT. You are likely to make the same number of tricks in 4H also, which is not enough.

b) 4H. You were never planning to play in 3NT. You bid 2NT, because you wanted to be in game if partner was maximum. Naturally, you are delighted that he has two of the top three trump honours, and game now looks excellent.

STRONG 2 OPENING BIDS

If you pick up a Strong 2 in hearts or spades, you will have to find an alternative. It must be said that these alternatives are not quite as accurate as the old-fashioned Strong 2 Opener but, frankly, that is a very small price to pay for being able to cause disruption so regularly with your Weak 2 openings.

Again, there are many alternative methods, but the one below keeps most of your existing Acol bidding intact.

2NT   remains a strong balanced hand of 21-22 points (20 points, if the hand contains tens or a 5-card suit).

2C   remains the Acol game-force, which is particularly powerful with the new responses.

2D   becomes a bid which shows a Strong 2 in any one of the four suits. Over partner's response, you rebid to indicate your suit.

Obviously this means that when your suit is clubs, diamonds, or hearts, you cannot reveal your suit until the 3-level. For this reason, you should keep Strong Two Openers fully up to strength. Minimum 8 playing trick hands can be opened at the 1-level quite safely, and then followed up with a jump rebid, or a forcing rebid in another suit.

Although this is slightly limiting, when you consider how rarely you pick up a Strong 2, compared to the frequency of a Weak 2, hopefully you will see that this is a small sacrifice.

Some players agree that a 2D opening, followed by a 2NT rebid, shows a balanced 19-20 points. This is a bad idea. The point of opening at the 2-level is to avoid missing game if partner would have passed a 1-level opening bid. It is extremely unlikely that you have a game opposite a balanced 19-20 points if partner has 5 points or fewer.

A more sensible arrangement would be to have the 2NT rebid showing a strong 4-4-4-1 hand. However, that is a matter for further partnership research.

Responding to 2D

You always respond with a relay bid of 2H, unless you have a suit so good that you wish to suggest it immediately as an alternative trump suit. Such a suit would almost always contain two of the top three honours.

Partner opens 2D:

a)	b)	c)	d)
♠ 632	♠ A97	♠ 432	♠ KQJ987
♡ Q2	♡ K82	♡ J83	♡ 5
◊ J8432	◊ AJ3	◊ AJ6432	◊ 753
♣ Q32	♣ Q987	♣ 2	♣ K98

a)   2H. You have to respond, and the relay promises no values.

b)   2H. Whichever suit your partner names, you will be interested in a slam. For the moment however, you just want to know which suit it is.

c)   2H. Your diamonds are not good enough to suggest as trumps. Besides, if you respond 3D, and your partner's suit is clubs, he will be forced to 4-level.

d)   2S. You have an excellent suit and, if your partner's suit is hearts, the hand may well play much better in spades. Get this message across straight away.

Let's look at how the auction might run on a couple of hands:

a)

W	E
♠ AKQJ98	♠ 4
♡ 43	♡ AJ985
◇ AQJ	◇ K32
♣ 82	♣ J763

W	E
2D	2H
2S	3H
3S	4S

b)

W	E
♠ K3	♠ AQJ987
♡ KQJ987	♡ A
◇ A92	◇ 653
♣ AQ	♣ 983

W	E
2D	2S
4NT	5S
7NT	

a) East makes the relay in response to West's 2D opener. West shows his suit with 2S, which can be passed by responder if he has a very poor hand.

   East's 3H bid shows a good 5-card, or poor quality 6-card suit, which cannot be headed by two of the top three honours, or he would have bid 3H on the first round. When West rebids 3S, confirming no support for hearts, East settles for game.

b) East breaks the relay to show his alternative trump suit, which must be 6 cards of excellent quality. With a fit in spades, and a hand full of controls (aces and kings), West wades into Roman Key Card (see page 181) Blackwood and, upon discovering two aces and the trump queen, can bid the grand slam with confidence.

DEFENDING AGAINST
WEAK 2 OPENINGS

The problem for the opponents of a Weak 2 opener is that
it has used up two levels of bidding. This is your vital
bidding space squandered by the opposition. Although
you may be able to extract a penalty, most of the time
your opponents will have eight trumps between them, and
your penalty will be no greater than if you had made a
part-score. That is fine, of course, if you are able to judge
that part-score was the limit of your combined hands, but
there is no satisfaction from gaining +100 on a hand when
you could have made +620 in game. So, generally, your
intention will be to end up playing the hand at the right
level and in the correct denomination.

There are several conventional defences to Weak 2s,
but they are not really to be recommended. It is much better to use standard methods, similar to those used over a
1-level opening, and add just one gadget, "Lebensohl",
which will buy back some of the bidding space you have
lost.

Double
This should always be played for take-out, both immediately over the opening bid and in the balancing position.
The requirements are exactly the same as over a 1-level
opening bid, with one exception: it may be necessary for
you to double with a 2-suited hand – something we would
never consider at the 1-level.

RHO opens 2H:

a) ♠ QJ63   b) ♠ K97   c) ♠ K986
    ♡ 3   ♡ 92   ♡ 85
    ◇ KJ104   ◇ A52   ◇ AQJ109
    ♣ AJ98   ♣ AK432   ♣ A3

a) Double. A minimum, well-shaped, take-out double.

b) Double. Far from ideal shape, but double is much
   more flexible than overcalling 3C.

c) Double. Quite unsuitable shape, but we have too good
   a hand to pass. Overcalling 3D by-passes 2S which
   may be our best spot. At least double keeps the
   options open. If partner responds 3C, we will bid 3D,
   and that will show a 2-suited hand with the two suits
   other than clubs, namely diamonds and spades.

The fact that Weak 2s are so tough to defend against
proves how effective a pre-empt they are. They cause a
whole bunch of trouble, for comparatively little risk. Now,
here's the next nightmare they present:

*RHO opens 2H, you double, partner responds 3D. What
do you bid now?*

    ♠   A1062
    ♡   Q2
    ◇   AQJ10
    ♣   A85

Your hand is a good deal stronger than it might have been,
but partner has responded to your double at the lowest
available level, and may therefore be staring at a
Yarborough. Equally, he may have 10-count with a heart
stopper, and 3NT will be cold.

    The simple fact is that because your RHO opened 2H
rather than 1H, your partner has lost a round of bidding.

Over 1H doubled, he could have bid 2D with 0-7 points, and 3D with 8-10, or thereabouts, and you would have known whether to continue bidding or not. Now, you are just guessing . . .

What about this?

RHO opens 2S, you double, partner responds 3H. What do you bid now?

    ♠   2
    ♡   AQ92
    ◊   AQ76
    ♣   KQ85

You have no idea whether partner has no points or 10 points; whether he has a 4-card or a 5-card suit. It is just a guess whether to bid 4H or not. What is more, if you do bid 4H, and partner has a very weak hand, you may get doubled by your LHO. He can be sitting with a very strong hand with short spades, waiting for his opponents to go overboard. Because the strong hand is then sitting over your good hand, the penalties can be enormous. Thankfully, there is a gadget to add to your system which buys back some of the space the Weak 2s have stolen from you.

Lebensohl
This convention was not invented for this bidding situation, but it works a treat.

- In response to your partner's take-out double of a Weak 2, if you bid 2NT, you tell your partner that you hold a minimum response.
- Over your 2NT, the doubler is forced to rebid 3C. If this is your suit, you just pass; if it is not, you then bid your own suit at the 3-level and your partner knows that you have a terrible hand.

- If you do not bid the Lebensohl 2NT, but respond at the 3-level, that shows that you have a decent hand with the values to bid at the 3-level, usually about 8-11 points.

- Of course this means that you cannot bid 2NT to play, but that is a small loss. 2NT is almost never the right contract – it is either too much or too little. If you think that NTs is the right spot, bid 3NT immediately.

LHO opens 2S, your partner doubles, RHO passes.

a)	b)	c)	d)
♠ 9863	♠ A97	♠ AQ6	♠ 9432
♡ J876	♡ AJ642	♡ 85	♡ 8
◇ 432	◇ Q52	◇ AQ109	◇ 83
♣ 98	♣ 32	♣ 9873	♣ QJ9832

a) 2NT – Lebensohl. Partner will rebid 3C, and you then bid 3H. This shows a minimum response and partner should pass.

b) 3H. This shows a hand where you want to play in 3H opposite a minimum take-out double from partner.

c) 3NT. You would like to bid 2NT, but you can't anymore, because it would be Lebensohl. At least you will have a very good idea as to the distribution of your opponents' cards, and the likely position of the outstanding high cards. The extra information from the bidding may well make up for what might be a shortage of high card points.

d) 2NT – Lebensohl. Partner will rebid 3C and you will pass, confirming a very weak hand with a club suit.

Having added Lebensohl to our system, we can return to the earlier examples and see if we still have the same problems.

RHO opens 2H, you double, partner responds 2NT, you rebid 3C as required, and partner bids 3D. What do you bid now?

♠ A1062
♡ Q2
◊ AQJ10
♣ A85

Now you know that partner is weak, game looks very unlikely, and you can pass without worrying that you have been conned out of a big plus score.

Before the introduction of Lebensohl, your partner had responded 3D, and we had no idea whether he was weak or strong. If he bid 3D now, that would show strength (probably about 8-11 points), and we could rebid 3H, asking for help in hearts for 3NT.

What about this?

RHO opens 2S, you double, partner responds 3H. What do you bid now?

♠ 2
♡ AQ92
◊ AQ76
♣ KQ85

Partner has not used Lebensohl, so he has some values. We can definitely bid 4H, because we know he must hold at least 8 or 9 points.

There is nothing to stop the responder jumping to 4H if he has a good hand. Lebensohl is just there to bring back the 2-level minimum responses that you would have had if the opening bid had been at the 1-level.

You do not need Lebensohl if you are bidding spades over a take-out double of 2H. In that situation, you can bid 2S with a lousy hand, jump to 3S with a reasonable hand, and go straight to game with a good hand. You don't need Lebensohl because you still had the 2-level response available to show the lousy hand.

You should use double for take-out over Weak 2s even after a barrage sequence like 2S – 3S or 2H – 4H. Obviously, the higher you force your partner to bid, the better the hand you will require, in terms of points, texture of suits and general shape of hand.

Overcalling a Weak 2 Opener

Because double will show a 3-suiter or a 2-suiter, all 1-suited hands must be shown with an overcall:

- Simple overcall. This will usually be at the 3-level, so you will need a good quality suit, usually of 6-cards, and close to opening hand values. You might bid 2S over 2H with a good quality 5-card suit, but even that is quite risky.

- Jump Overcall. The one you are most likely to make will be 3S over a Weak 2H opening. This should guarantee a 6-card suit, and be played strongly, showing a hand of at least 7 playing tricks.

- 2NT. Not the Unusual NT over a Weak 2, but a natural overcall showing 17-20 points, with at least one stopper in the opponent's suit. The wide range makes this a flexible bid, but difficult for partner to judge in response.

  Again, the Weak 2 has cost us a round of bidding, and we are suffering for it.

Whatever gadgets you play in response to an opening bid of 2NT should be played here, including Stayman (or Modified Baron) and Transfers.

- 3NT. A natural overcall, when you want to play in 3NT. This is often based on a good hand with a long minor suit which you hope will run to produce tricks.

- Cue-bid. There are many different agreements which you can have for this bid. I recommend that it is a try for 3NT asking partner to bid 3NT if he has a solid stopper in the opponent's suit. This allows you to bully your way into 3NT with long minor suits, which is quite a frequent hand pattern after a Weak 2.

Let's see these bids in action.

Your RHO opens 2S

a)	b)	c)	d)
♠ KJ6	♠ K97	♠ 86	♠ 2
♡ AQ3	♡ A9	♡ K8	♡ 85
◇ KJ4	◇ Q5	◇ AKQJ865	◇ KQJ93
♣ A983	♣ AKQJ32	♣ A4	♣ AQJ98

a) 2NT. Natural, showing a balanced hand with 17-20 points.

b) 3NT. If you add the average Weak 2 point-count of 7 points to your 19 points, that makes 26. Therefore, your partner is expected to hold, on average, half the remaining 14 points. If he has 7 points, you should waltz home in 3NT.

c) 3S. This cue-bid says that you want to play in 3NT if partner has a solid stop in spades. If he does, he bids

3NT; if he doesn't, he bids his long suit, and you will have to bid your own long suit. When your partner turns up with ♠A and not much else, you will score tremendously well for being in 3NT.

d) Double, 3D, or even pass, but not 2NT. There is no Unusual No-trump over Weak 2s. Double is far from great. Partner will bid hearts, and you will have to re-bid clubs to show a minor 2-suiter.

All these bids should mean the same in the balancing position also, but be aware that the partner of the Weak 2 opener may hold a strong hand, with a shortage in his partner's suit, and he will be well placed to defend against bidding excesses.

Lastly, it is worth remembering that, as with Weak 3 pre-empts, the bidding is tipping you off that there is some funny distribution around. You should not be surprised if suits break badly and, for that reason, do not stretch to bid games or slams unless you have plenty of trumps. 8-card fits play notoriously badly after pre-empts, when the trumps split 4-1 or 5-0. You have been warned . . .

ADVANCED RESPONSES TO 2C

When partner opens 2C he holds either a balanced hand with 23 points or more, or a distributional hand with the potential for 10 playing tricks. In standard Acol, the responses do not take into account the fact that the vast majority of 2C openers are made on 1 or 2-suited distributional hands with pronounced shortages in the remaining suits. Because of this, the opener is not generally interested in the number of points held by the responder, but rather where any source of tricks may lie.

These improved responses to 2C reflect these needs, while making all auctions after 2C easier to develop.

In response to a 2C opening bid:

- 2H is an instant double negative, denying any cue-biddable values (aces and kings) and showing a very weak hand with a point range of 0-4 points. Indeed, you would only be as strong as 4 points if your hand contained all four jacks – useless cards for a partner hopeful of a slam.

- 2D becomes a relay bid, promising 4 points or more, but denying a definite source of tricks in any one suit. There is no upper limit in points for this bid. If the opener rebids 2NT, it will be easy to make a limit or quantitative raise. If the opener rebids a suit, and subsequently signs off, you can re-open the bidding with a cue-bid or further raise to indicate extra values.

- 2S, 3C, 3D, and higher are positive responses, showing a 5-card suit or longer, headed by two of the top three honours. When you make one of these bids, your partner will know that there is a reliable source of tricks available in that suit.

- 2NT shows a positive response in hearts, as 2H is now taken as the instant double negative response.

Notice that you have lost the old-fashioned 2NT and 3NT responses to show a scattering of points. These were quite unnecessary, as it was impossible to judge the value of your hand until you knew what type of 2C opener your partner was holding.

These responses also have an important and beneficial side effect on the opener's rebids:

W	E
2C	2H
2NT	

still shows a balanced 23-24 points and is completely non-forcing. Whereas:

W	E
2C	2D
2NT	

shows 23 points or more, and is 100% forcing. This is because, when the responder bids 2D, he is promising some values (4 points+), and therefore game should always be on opposite a balanced 23 points.

Additionally, this means that the 2C opener does not need to rebid 3NT with 25-27 points, or even more NTs with more points than that. He can just rebid 2NT, knowing that partner has to bid on, and that he can use all the gadgets you play opposite a 2NT opener in this position also. This gives responder room to use Stayman (or Modified Baron), Transfers, and anything else you fancy.

The 2C opener can also distinguish between high and low quality suits in responder's hand:

W	E
2C	2S

promises a 5-card suit or longer headed by two of the top three honours.

W	E
2C	2D
2NT	3S

as the positive response was not given, this must show a 5-card suit without two of the top three honours. (If you were playing transfers you would bid 3H here.)

Following a 2D relay response and suit agreement, the 2C opener can make a mild slam try – stopping at the 5-level if necessary – safe in the knowledge that his partner holds some values. Over a 2H double negative, the opener can often rule out a slam contract immediately knowing that his partner cannot hold any aces or kings. This way, he will not need to risk higher levels for slam investigation.

Here are some hands to demonstrate the principles:

a)

W	E
♠ KQJ3	♠ 10984
♡ AKQ	♡ J85
◇ AK3	◇ QJ87
♣ A82	♣ J5

W	E
2C	2D
2NT	3C
3S	4S

b)

W	E
♠ AQJ9876	♠ 3
♡ AK5	♡ J62
◇ A2	◇ 87653
♣ A	♣ J642

W	E
2C	2H
4S	

a) East's 2D relay promises some values, so West can rebid 2NT, which is now forcing. This allows East to use Stayman and locate the 4-4 spade fit. Even if West decides that his hand is worth a slam try and he bids on, 5S will still make.

Significantly, in traditional Acol, West would have had to rebid 3NT, East would have passed and, on the likely club lead, 3NT could be defeated.

b) East's instant double negative 2H immediately tells West that there will be no slam available as East cannot hold ♠K or ◇K (he could hold ♡Q, but nothing much else). Instead of agonizing over a possible slam, West can sign off with his safe 4S game. 5S is very unlikely to make, yet most Wests would have found it irresistible to make a slam try had they not known East was so weak.

These improved responses can stop you not only from overbidding, they can also propel you into the right slam contract without any of the associated angst and finger-biting . . .

c)

W	E
♠ AQ3	♠ K94
♡ KQ7	♡ A85
◇ AKQ86	◇ 1094
♣ A2	♣ Q864

W	E
2C	2D
2NT	4NT
6NT	

d) **W**

♠ KJ3
♥ AKQJ76
♦ AQ9
♣ A

E

♠ AQ962
♥ 92
♦ 8532
♣ J2

W	E
2C	2S
7NT	

c) East makes the 2D relay because, although he holds a very good hand opposite a 2C opener, he has no particular source of tricks. When his partner rebids 2NT, showing 23 points+, he makes a quantitative raise to 4NT. As the opener's range is most often going to be 23-26 points, West accepts the slam invitation courtesy of his 24 points, plus his very important 5-card diamond suit.

d) This is a real hand from a national event. My partner and I were not only one of the few pairs to reach 7NT, but it took us only three bids! East's positive response of 2S promised two of the top three honours and a 5-card suit or longer. West could count 13 tricks unless the heart suit split horrendously, and he waited not a moment longer to bid the top contract.

Keeping the positive responses to two of the top three honours is slightly restrictive but, and it is a big but, because it is so precise you will find that the positive response makes your life very simple, and you can bid grand slams with confidence. Nothing does partnership confidence more good than a couple of well-bid slam hands.

MODIFIED BARON OR
5-CARD MAJOR STAYMAN

Whatever you call it, it is a very useful convention to have at your disposal.

In modern Acol, you require a 6-card suit to open a Strong 2, or 2D if you are playing Weak 2s. So, it is quite in order to open 2NT (or rebid 2NT in the sequence 2C-2D-2NT) with a hand including a 5-card major suit. Modified Baron allows the responder to bid 2NT to check for an 8-card fit in the majors, by searching for both a 4-4 fit and also a 3-5 fit.

Modified Baron therefore replaces Stayman opposite an opening bid of 2NT, as well as opposite:

- a protective overcall of 2NT;

- a 2NT overcall of a Weak 2 opener;

- a 2NT rebid in the sequence 2C-2D-2NT.

The Modified Baron Bid
A response of 3C to 2NT is Modified Baron.

You require only enough points to make game a possibility, and you can use the convention on any hand containing a 3 or 4-card major suit. You should not use the convention on hands containing a 5-card major suit, as this should be shown in the first place, either naturally or by using transfers.

The one exception will be when you hold five spades and four hearts, as this combination cannot be shown below 3NT, even using transfers.

Responses to Modified Baron

In response to 3C:

3H/3S show a 5-card suit.

3D denies a 5-card major suit, but promises either a 4-card heart suit, or a 3 or 4-card spade suit.

3NT shows no interest in the majors whatsoever, specifically no more than a 3-card heart suit and a 2-card spade suit.

After a 3NT response, there can be no 8-card fit in a major suit, so responder will pass or make a quantitative or limit raise in NTs.

Additionally, as the opener holds no more than five cards in the major suits, he is marked with length in the minors. This information may help you to reach a minor suit game or slam.

a)
W	E		W	E
♠ KJ732	♠ Q54		2NT	3C
♡ A3	♡ 85		3S	4S
◇ AQ6	◇ KJ92			
♣ AK2	♣ 8754			

b)
W	E		W	E
♠ A7	♠ K982		2NT	3C
♡ AQ10	♡ KJ62		3NT	4NT
◇ KQ875	◇ AJ3		6NT	
♣ AQ10	♣ 95			

a) East uses Modified Baron to check for a 3-5 fit in spades. When West confirms that he holds a 5-card spade suit, East raises to game. 4S should make comfortably, whereas 3NT should be defeated on the likely heart lead.

b) East uses Modified Baron just as he would Stayman. When West denies any interest in the majors, East makes his quantitative raise to 4NT, inviting partner to bid 6NT with a maximum. West's 5-card suit and two tens make 6NT a good bet.

After the 3D response, the convention takes on its Baron form:

1. If the 3C bidder does not hold a 4-card major suit, he will settle for 3NT or bid on in NTs.

2. If the 3C bidder holds one or more 4-card major suits, he now bids his suit(s) in ascending order. If, at any time, a 4-4 fit is found, game or slam can be investigated.

3. If the 3C bidder holds five spades and four hearts (the one time he uses Modified Baron with a 5-card major), he first bids 3H. If the 2NT opener denies 4-card support by rebidding 3NT, the responder can now convert to 4S, knowing that his partner holds 3-card spade support.

c)

W	E		W	E
♠ KJ73	♠ 54		2NT	3C
♡ A32	♡ KQ85		3D	3H
◇ A6	◇ J8732		3S	3NT
♣ AKQ2	♣ J5			

d)

W	E		W	E
♠ A76	♠ KQ832		2NT	3C
♡ AK5	♡ J962		3D	3H
◊ KQJ8	◊ 953		3NT	4S
♣ A43	♣ 2			

c) West responds 3D to East's Modified Baron enquiry, showing a 4-card heart suit or a 3 or 4-card spade suit. East shows his 4-card heart suit, West his 4-card spade suit and, with no fit in the majors, East settles for 3NT.

d) East responds with Modified Baron to check for both a 4-4 heart fit and for a 5-3 or 5-4 spade fit. When East responds 3D, showing either a 4-card heart suit or a 3 or 4-card spade suit, East checks first for a 4-4 heart fit by bidding his heart suit. When West denies 4-card heart or spade support, East knows that West must hold 3-card spade support, or he would have responded 3NT to his Modified Baron enquiry initially. So, East converts to 4S, which is the superior contract.

Further Bids

Once you have established an 8-card fit, a new suit at the 4-level or 5-level by the 3C bidder is a cue-bid, searching for a slam.

e)

W	E		W	E
♠ Q3	♠ A4		2NT	3C
♡ A932	♡ KQ85		3D	3H
◊ AQ6	◊ K32		4H	4S etc
♣ AKQ2	♣ 9875			

e) Having found the 4-4 heart fit, East begins to investigate slam possibilities by cue-bidding ♠A. West, with a hand heavy with aces and kings, will surely continue to cue-bid, or utilize Blackwood, preferably Roman Key Card Blackwood.

Cue-bidding at the 4-level can begin immediately if the 2NT opener shows a 5-card major suit, as in this sequence:

f) W   E

♠ AQ976	♠ KJ2
♡ KQ5	♡ A642
◇ AK4	◇ 93
♣ K6	♣ A982

W	E
2NT	3C
3S	4C etc

f) When the opener shows either 5-card major, a new suit by the responder is always a cue-bid, showing slam interest. Here 7S is an excellent contract, whereas 7NT is unlikely to succeed. Because suit agreement has been found so effortlessly, cue-bidding can begin at a lower level, and there is a chance the grand slam can be reached.

Even the 2NT opener can cue-bid to show a particularly suitable hand, as here:

g) W   E

♠ AQ93	♠ KJ65
♡ A7	♡ K85
◇ KQJ	◇ A832
♣ AJ85	♣ 63

W	E
2NT	3C
3D	3S
4C etc	

g) When East shows a 4-card spade suit, if West did not hold support, he would bid 3NT. Therefore, this sequence shows that West has good quality 4-card spade support, probably maximum points, but above all, a slam-oriented hand containing good controls (aces and kings). The 4C bid shows ♣A.

Notice that, because West's cue-bid is below the level of game, if East were not interested in slam, he could now sign off in 4S. As it is, he will gladly co-operate by cue-bidding his ◊A, and 6S should be reached without much difficulty.

The 2NT opener, who has made a limit bid, can never cue-bid beyond game unless the responder has shown some interest in slam. It must always be the decision of the responder whether to hunt for a slam.

TRANSFERS, WITH ADVANCED RESPONSES OF "BREAKING" AND "BOUNCING"

In themselves, transfers are not particularly competitive in nature but, as you will see, there are definite obstructive influences on low-level competitive bidding. The most important reason for transfers, however, is that they allow you to bid much more accurately in all instances over NT openings, as well as some NT overcalls and rebids.

If you play transfers in response to a 1NT opener, you should seriously consider playing them in response to all these bids as well:

- a 2NT opener;

- a 1NT overcall, both in the direct position and the protective position;

- a protective 2NT overcall;

- a 2NT overcall of a Weak 2 bid;

- a 2NT rebid, after a 2C opener.

Major-suit Transfers

1NT - 2D   promises a 5-card heart suit or longer, with an unlimited point-count. Opener must rebid 2H (unless suitable for a break or bounce).

1NT - 2H   promises a 5-card spade suit or longer, with an unlimited point-count. Opener must rebid 2S (unless suitable for a break or bounce).

Remember:

- once the 1NT opener has completed the transfer, all further bids are natural;
- if the responder passes the completed transfer, this indicates a weak take-out situation;
- if he bids a new suit, showing at least 5-4 distribution, this is forcing to game;
- a transfer, followed by NT rebid, shows the standard limit raise, including a 5-card major suit.

a)

W	E
♠ K2	♠ AJ987
♡ A832	♡ KQ5
◇ A86	◇ J92
♣ J1097	♣ 54

W	E
1NT	2H
2S	2NT
NB	

b)

W	E
♠ 652	♠ 3
♡ A4	♡ K9872
◇ KQ87	◇ AJ32
♣ A743	♣ KQ5

W	E
1NT	2D
2H	3D
4D	5D

a) East's 2H transfer promises a 5-card spade suit or longer, West completes the transfer, and East now shows a balanced hand containing 11-12 points. With a minimum and only 2-card spade support, West can pass.

This is why transfers were invented. Playing natural methods, East has either to make a game-forcing 3S bid, misuse Stayman to make an invitational spade

bid, or ignore spades altogether and bid 2NT immediately. The transfer allows both the point-count, and
the 5-card major to be shown, with the resulting 2NT
the safest contract.

b) East's 2D shows a 5-card heart suit or longer and,
over West's completion of the transfer, East bids a
natural and forcing 3D, showing 5-4 in hearts and
diamonds. East should not show a second suit unless
his values are concentrated in those two suits and
there are gaps in the remaining suits for NTs. West
holds poor spades and only a single stopper in clubs,
and therefore supports diamonds, allowing East-West
to find their best game contract.

> The natural Acol sequence of 1NT - 3H - 3NT would
> not be a success.

These transfers are played in the same way over a 2NT
bid also.

Having transferred, if the responder bids his suit again –
this time naturally, it promises a 6-card suit. So,

c) W   E

  ♠ K2   ♠ AQJ987
  ♡ A832   ♡ K5
  ◇ KJ52   ◇ 643
  ♣ J85   ♣ 97

W	E
1NT	2H
2S	3S
NB	

d) W   E

  ♠ K62   ♠ AQ7532
  ♡ K76   ♡ 93
  ◇ QJ83   ◇ AK
  ♣ K43   ♣ 872

W	E
1NT	2H
2S	4S

c) Without transfers, East would have to decide whether to have a punt at game or settle for a weak take-out. Using transfers, however, the raise to 3S by East shows an invitational hand with a 6-card spade suit. Although West has good cards for a suit contract, he holds the minimum number of both points and spades, and correctly decides to pass.

d) Here, the advantage is merely in having West play the hand, so that his bare kings can be protected from the opening lead. 4S may still fail, but then it was almost certainly going off anyway. Played from the West side, the chances of success and of overtricks are greatly improved.

"Breaking" and "Bouncing"

These actions should be taken by the 1NT or 2NT bidder to show that his hand is particularly suitable for playing in the suit shown by the transfer bidder. If you already play transfers and you wonder why I am introducing more new-fangled complications, let me reassure you that these responses were part of the original transfers convention being written about in the 1950s. No top player would dream of playing transfers without these excellent additional responses, and neither should you.

You open 1NT, partner responds 2D (transfer):

a) ♠ 63   b) ♠ KJ97
   ♡ KJ97   ♡ 92
   ◇ AKJ10   ◇ QJ2
   ♣ Q82   ♣ AJ32

a) With your maximum opener, you are delighted to hear that your partner holds a 5-card heart suit, not only because you hold 4-card support but also because in a heart contract, your small doubleton spade has suddenly become a great asset.

b) You are minimum, you have no support for hearts, and you are quite probably wishing that you had never bid in the first place.

Do you not agree that it would be ridiculous to make the same rebid on both these hands? In a) the opener is delighted with the way the auction is developing; in b) he wants to crawl under a stone.

The good news is that we do not have to respond in the same way on both hands.

"Breaking", having bid 1NT

This is the stronger of the two actions, to be used when you hold a maximum hand for your NT bid, 4-card support for the major suit shown, and a working doubleton. Such a doubleton will not contain the queen, which is more likely to be useful in NTs.

In these circumstances, instead of merely completing the transfer, you bid the suit in which you hold the doubleton:

W	E		W	E
♠ AQ93	♠ K8652		1NT	2H
♡ K32	♡ A5		3C	4S
◊ AJ108	◊ 32			
♣ 75	♣ A632			

West shows that his hand is particularly suitable for playing with spades as trumps by not completing the transfer, but breaking it. He bids 3C to show that his doubleton is in the club suit. East, initially doubtful about his game prospects, now knows that his partner's hand fits very well with his own, and he jumps to game.

Having broken the transfer, if the responder returns to the trump suit at the lowest available level, this indicates that he held a weak take-out hand, and does not wish to take the bidding any higher.

Do not be concerned that you will take the level of the bidding too high by breaking the transfer. Even if partner holds a Yarborough, as he has five trumps and you have 4-card support, you hold nine cards between you. The Total Trumps Principle confirms that you have therefore competed to the correct level. Your opponents, who may hold the clear majority of the points, will now have to enter the bidding at the 3-level or higher. This is just one of the competitive side-effects of playing transfers.

W	E
♠ J75	♠ 64
♡ KQJ7	♡ 109865
◇ 42	◇ Q973
♣ AK75	♣ 63

W	E
1NT	2D
3D	3H

East signs off in 3H after the transfer break to indicate a weak take-out hand. Although 3H will fail, probably only by one trick, the opponents have a certain spade part-score and possibly even game.

Breaking the transfer will never take you past the 3-level sign-off and, as you have 4-card support and a useful doubleton, the nine trick level will always be a good competitive level to have reached. As well as being a sound competitive manoeuvre, and helping to bid slim game contracts, the break can also reassure partner that a slam is a good prospect:

W	E
♠ AJ93	♠ KQ8652
♡ 92	♡ AK85
◇ A832	◇ K9
♣ AJ7	♣ 6

W	E
1NT	2H
3H	4NT
5S	7S

Initially, East may sniff the possibility of a small slam but, when West breaks the transfer to show 4-card spade support, maximum values, and a doubleton heart, East will feel far more confident, knowing that his two small hearts can be safely ruffed, and that opener has excellent trump support. When West shows three aces (using standard Blackwood), East realizes that 7S is an excellent contract, and can bid the grand slam with confidence.

"Breaking", having bid 2NT

Having opened 2NT (or rebid or overcalled 2NT in the agreed situations), you should break the transfer whenever you have a maximum hand with 4-card support. Instead of breaking to a doubleton, it is more sensible to break to the suit where you hold your best outside values.

This is because, as you hold such a strong hand, your partner is more likely to want to know where your strength lies, than whether you happen to hold a doubleton.

So, you might achieve a sequence like this:

W	E
♠ AQJ2	♠ K9873
♡ A93	♡ K65
◇ KQ103	◇ AJ97
♣ AJ	♣ 3

W	E
2NT	3H
4D	

West breaks the transfer to show good 4-card spade support, and a source of tricks in diamonds. East's borderline slam hand has been transformed by the knowledge that West has good diamonds, as well as spade support, and East should have no difficulty in investigating and bidding 6S, or even the far-fetched, but making, 7D.

With minimum 2NT hands containing 4-card support, you should always bounce in response to the transfer.

Bouncing

This is the competitive, barrage-forming response to the transfer, where we bounce to one level higher than usual in the auction, to be made on hands which are not good enough to break the transfer, but still contain high quality 4-card support for partner's suit.

The knowledge that you hold 4-card support may be enough to persuade your partner to try for a slim game or slam. However, in this situation, you and your partner hold nine cards between you, and you are therefore safe to compete to the 3-level, even if your partner was planning to make a weak take-out.

Because you will either hold a minimum 1NT opener, or a hand which does not contain a working doubleton (or you would have broken the transfer), you should be aware both of your hand make-up, and also of the vulnerability. Whilst you would like to obstruct the opposition, you do not want to force them into doubling you because they have no other option available to them.

You should bounce when:

- your side is not vulnerable, and particularly when your opponents are;

- your values are concentrated in your long suit, and

not when scattered around the hand as these are useful in defence;

- your values are aces and kings, rather than queens and jacks which are, again, more useful in defence.

You should not bounce when:

- you are vulnerable and your opponents are not;

- your hand is 4-3-3-3, minimum, and rich in queens, jacks and tens;

- your four trumps are poor quality.

Love All. You open 1NT, partner responds 2H, transfer:

a) ♠ QJ63   b) ♠ AKQ9   c) ♠ 5432
   ♡ 32   ♡ K43   ♡ KJ5
   ◇ AJ74   ◇ 952   ◇ KQJ9
   ♣ A98   ♣ 432   ♣ Q10

a) 3S. You are minimum, so you cannot break. However, your hand is very useful in spades so you should bounce.

b) 3S. A minimum again – and you were quite right to open 1NT. Now, you must bounce because, if partner was planning a weak take-out, 3S will stop your opponents bidding their making part-score or game.

c) 2S. Lousy trumps and good defensive tricks in the outside suits.

A quick word about a couple of these phrases:

- a "maximum hand" does not really mean every hand with 14pts, but hands containing a preponderance of aces and kings – which are good for suit contracts –

rather than queens and jacks – which are better for NT contracts.

- a "working doubleton" means a doubleton suitable for making ruffs. Best of all would be a small doubleton that is clearly ideal for a suit contract and a worry for NTs. In fact, almost all doubletons, apart from those containing the queen will do. AQ, KQ, QJ, Q10, and Qx are all likely to be of more use in a NT contract than in a suit. Whilst you would not break the transfer to this suit, you may still decide to bounce.

Hence:

You open 1NT, partner bids 2H, transfer:

a)	b)	c)	d)
♠ AJ98	♠ KQ97	♠ 9863	♠ J642
♡ 93	♡ A986	♡ K5	♡ AQJ
◇ A1094	◇ A2	◇ QJ104	◇ KJ83
♣ A42	♣ 432	♣ AKJ	♣ Q10

a) Break to 3H. Only 13 points, but what a 13 points! Excellent trumps and three aces. This may be an average 1NT hand in NTs, but it is a maximum if spades (or diamonds) are trumps. Partner will know you have a fit in spades and go to game.

b) Break to 3D. Again only 13 points, and again a hand that is worth much more now that spades are going to be trumps. No wasted queens or jacks in the side suits, make this hand perfect for a break.

c) Bounce to 3S. You may have 14 points and a doubleton, but this is not nearly as suitable as the two previous hands. All your values are in the outside suits, and the diamonds are lovely for NTs, but possibly useless in a spade contract.

d) 2S – maybe 3S if not vulnerable, on a sunny Friday. Not worth a break because the doubleton club queen does not count as a doubleton suitable for making ruffs.

Any new suit introduced after a bounce or a break will be a cue-bid, beginning the investigation for a possible slam.

3-level responses to 1NT

Because 3H and 3S are no longer needed as game-forcing bids, you can agree to attach a new meaning to this sequence. The simplest method is to standardize all 3-level responses to 1NT, both in the minors and the majors, making them mild slam tries.

a)

W	E
♠ K2	♠ AQJ543
♡ QJ32	♡ K86
◇ KJ86	◇ AQ2
♣ KJ7	♣ 5

W	E
1NT	3S
3NT	4S
NB	

b)

W	E
♠ A7	♠ 873
♡ Q105	♡ AK9764
◇ AK6	◇ 2
♣ 98743	♣ AKQ

W	E
1NT	3H
3S	4C
4D	4NT etc

a) East has a typically difficult decision. A good hand, but not really strong enough to risk the 5-level unless the 1NT opener shows some enthusiasm. Playing jumps to the 3-level as mild slam tries allows the 1NT opener to cue-bid immediately if he wants to co-operate with slam intentions, and to sign off in 3NT or 4-of-the-suit, if he is not interested.

Here, despite a nice feature in spades, West's aceless hand is clearly not slam orientated, so he rebids 3NT to show good cards in all the other suits. East decides to settle for 4S. Even 5S may be too much, if North-South are able to engineer a heart ruff.

b) This time, West loves the idea of a slam in hearts, as he holds nothing but pure control cards in the outside suits. He immediately cue-bids 3S, and East-West should now sail into their excellent 6H contract. Note that 3S cannot be a suit – a 1NT opener is not permitted to introduce new suits – any change of suit must be a cue-bid showing an excellent fit with partner.

Minor suit transfers

Playing major suit transfers releases the 2S response to 1NT, and this can now be used as a minor suit transfer. Again, there are many alternatives, but the best use is as a game-try with a 6-card minor suit.

When holding a 6-card minor suit with 9-11 points, you will want to be in 3NT whenever your partner holds a fit with that suit. However, if he holds no fit, 3C or 3D is likely to be the superior spot.

A response of 2S to 1NT requires the opener to transfer to 2NT, over which the responder shows his 6-card minor suit, which should be headed by either ace or king. If the opener believes that this suit will run – because he holds ace or king doubleton or any 3-card support – he bids 3NT; if he holds a small doubleton, he passes, leaving 3-of-the-minor as the final contract.

a)

W	E
♠ A82	♠ 43
♡ K832	♡ A6
◇ QJ3	◇ 872
♣ K75	♣ AQ9632

W	E
1NT	2S
2NT	3C
3NT	

b)   **W**   **E**

    ♠ K642   ♠ AJ3

    ♡ Q83   ♡ 74

    ◊ 62   ◊ KQ8543

    ♣ AKQ2   ♣ 76

W	E
1NT	2S
2NT	3D
NB	

a) East shows his 6-card club suit through the transfer sequence and West, with excellent support for clubs, rebids 3NT – a solid 23 point game.

b) Despite holding a maximum opener, West holds no fit with East's diamonds, and passes. 3NT is very unlikely to make, whilst 3D offers a very good opportunity of a plus score.

There are additional sequences which can be agreed following this minor suit transfer, but they deal with rare hand distributions and, in my experience, do not contribute to partnership harmony!

Weak take-outs in the minor suits

Finally, we must deal with the occasional need to make a weak take-out into a minor suit after partner's 1NT opener. Thankfully, this is a very simple matter, as we can treat the diamond suit in exactly the same way that we have behaved with clubs in standard Acol. To make a weak take-out then, we go through Stayman, so that:

1NT   2C

2D/H/S   3C   is a weak take-out into clubs,

and

1NT   2C

2H/S   3D   is a weak take-out into diamonds.

If your partner responds 2D, you can pass. Otherwise, as you are committing your side to the 3-level, despite weakness, you should ensure that you reserve this action for very weak hands, of no conceivable worth in NTs, containing a 6-card suit or longer.

Partner opens 1NT:

a)	b)	c)	d)
♠ 62	♠ 1097	♠ 86	♠ 92
♡ Q102	♡ 2	♡ 75	♡ 8532
◊ KJ764	◊ K52	◊ 9865432	◊ 5
♣ Q98	♣ AQJ832	♣ KQ	♣ QJ9876

a) Pass. All your values are suitable for NTs and there is no reason why 2D should be a better contract, let alone the 3D you will have to play in.

b) 2S. This is too strong for a weak take-out, and is suitable for a try for game via a minor suit transfer.

c) 2C, followed by 3D, unless partner responds 2D, when you can pass. This hand is certainly going to be more use in diamonds than in NTs, unless your partner holds the miracle hand. As there is a simple rule to cover this situation – "partner never holds the miracle hand if the thought has occurred to you that he might" – you can be safe in the knowledge that making a weak take-out will improve your final contract, and may inhibit the opposition from finding their major suit fit.

d) 2C. If partner happens to reply 2H, you've found your best spot. Failing that, 3C is likely to be marginally less awful than 1NT, and bidding Stayman may dissuade the opposition from investigating whether they hold a spade fit.

NEGATIVE DOUBLES

In the old days, if your RHO opened 1D and you doubled, it was for penalties. Very soon, players realised that there was not much call for making penalty doubles in this situation, and so the take-out double was invented which was far more useful.

In the same way, players have realised that playing this sequence as penalties is equally unlikely to be right:

N	E	S	W
–	1H	2C	Dbl

The number of situations where it is right to make a low-level penalty double on this type of auction is very small. However, the opponent's overcall has used up your bidding space, preventing you from describing your hand. Most particularly, if you hold a 4-card spade suit, you have now been prevented from showing it. This is where playing negative doubles is so useful: it gives you back the bidding space you have lost.

To play negative doubles then, you and your partner must agree that these doubles will be take-out, and not penalties. You must further agree to what level of the bidding you will have this understanding. Some pairs play that if the opponents' intervention is higher than 3D, your doubles should revert to penalties. An increasing number of experts feel that all doubles in this situation are negative (or at least value-showing) doubles.

The other consideration is at what level you cease to guarantee 4-card majors – both majors over 1C-1D, or the unbid major when the other has been bid? I recommend that you start by playing negative doubles up to and including the level of 3D, and that those doubles guarantee the other requisite major suit(s). Doubles beyond this level should be played as penalties.

As you become more confident in the use of negative doubles, your partnership can agree to play them at higher levels, when they indicate balanced hands, and suggest that your side holds the majority of points. This allows opener to consider converting the negative double to penalties by passing, unless he holds a distributional hand.

Because negative doubles are simply replacing bids at various levels, their point-counts correspond to the usual counts required:

- at the 1-level 6 points +

- at the 2-level 8/9 points +

- at the 3-level 10 points +

There is no upper limit for these point-counts, because the hands on which you make them are of unlimited strength, and reasonably unlimited distribution.

Getting your 4-card major into the auction

In simple terms, the negative double allows you to show your 4-card major suit when you have been prevented from doing so at the 1-level:

Partner opens 1C, RHO overcalls 1S:

a)	b)	c)	d)
♠ 62	♠ Q94	♠ 6	♠ 92
♡ KQ92	♡ A982	♡ AQ75	♡ KQ93
◇ J764	◇ K52	◇ 9432	◇ KJ532
♣ J98	♣ QJ8	♣ K964	♣ 92

a) Double. This shows a 4-card heart suit, and 6 points or more. It is simply as if you responded 1H to partner's 1C. Opener will rebid in just the same way.

b) Double. You might bid 2NT, but your spade stop is not good enough, and you miss the chance to show your 4-card heart suit. By doubling, you show the hearts, and you can follow up with NTs or, better still, a spade cue-bid asking for help in the suit, unless your partner supports hearts.

c) Double. Show your 4-card heart suit and then, unless partner supports you, support his clubs next time.

d) Double. Despite your 5-card diamond suit, you are not strong enough to show it at the 2-level and then bid hearts later on, so get the message about your 4-card heart suit across first.

This is no different from deciding what to respond to a 1C opening bid without the intervention. On these hands, you should certainly respond 1H because, if you don't show it now, it is likely to get lost later on. As a responder, your top priority is to show 4-card major suits at the 1-level, and you must strain to do so.

Because the negative double shows four cards in the unbid major, you can achieve greater descriptive accuracy with the spade suit in this situation:

Partner opens 1C, RHO overcalls 1H:

a) ♠ AJ98   b) ♠ AQ743
    ♡ 96   ♡ 982
    ◇ K764   ◇ Q52
    ♣ Q98   ♣ 32

a) Double – to show your 4-card spade suit.

b) 1S – which promises a 5-card spade suit.

When neither major has been bid, the negative double should show *both* 4-card majors:

Partner opens 1C, RHO overcalls 1D:

a)	♠ AQ62	b)	♠ A6432
	♡ KJ85		♡ KQ98
	◇ 763		◇ 52
	♣ 42		♣ Q2

a) Double – showing 4-4 in the majors.

b) 1S, followed by a heart bid to show 5-4 or longer.

Similarly, when both majors have been bid, the negative double shows *both* minors:

Partner opens 1H, RHO overcalls 1S:

a)	♠ 54	b)	♠ 97
	♡ 962		♡ Q2
	◇ KJ76		◇ AK852
	♣ AQ98		♣ QJ83

a) Double – showing 4-4 in the minors.

b) 2D, followed by 3C to show 5-4 or longer.

Opener's rebid after a Negative Double

You should always rebid as if your partner has bid the suit he is showing naturally. It is especially important to support partner if you have discovered a 4-4 major suit fit, even if you were a minimum opener because, if you delay in doing so, you may be pre-empted out of the auction by your opponents.

You open 1C, LHO overcalls 1S, partner doubles, RHO passes:

a)	♠ AQ	b)	♠ 432	c)	♠ 86
	♡ 92		♡ A982		♡ AQ
	◇ KJ42		◇ 7		◇ AQ32
	♣ AKQ98		♣ AKJ53		♣ KQ987

In each case, you rebid simply as if partner responded 1H – the 4-card suit he is promising:

a) 3NT. You have two spade stops, your partner has shown four hearts and at least 6 points, so make your natural rebid.

b) 2H. Support your partner. This is not a reverse, because you are supporting your partner, not introducing a new suit. With extra values, you could make limit raises in hearts to 3H or even 4H.

c) 2D. This is a reverse, forcing as usual, because you have introduced a new suit.

To see the full effect of the negative double, let's glance at a full deal:

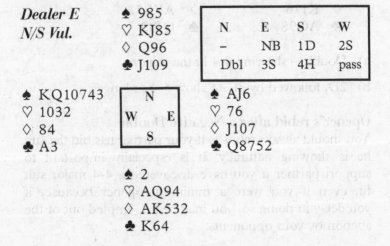

Dealer E
N/S Vul.

	♠ 985	
	♡ KJ85	
	◇ Q96	
	♣ J109	

N	E	S	W
–	NB	1D	2S
Dbl	3S	4H	pass

♠ KQ10743		♠ AJ6
♡ 1032		♡ 76
◇ 84		◇ J107
♣ A3		♣ Q8752

	♠ 2
	♡ AQ94
	◇ AK532
	♣ K64

Without the negative double, North would have been unable to bid anything after West's aggressive Weak Jump Overcall. Over East's 3S, South would then have had to decide whether it was worth the risk of a high-level take-out double. If he decided against it, East-West would have got out for one down in 3S, when North-South could have reached a cold game contract.

However, playing negative doubles, North could show his 4-card heart suit so that, even when East bid 3S, South could be pretty confident about bidding on to game.

The key here is that as modern bidding introduces more and more ways of using up bidding space, we must try to counter the attack with bids which give us back some of our lost ground. The negative double is a vital weapon against overcalls, weak jump overcalls and barrages.

Penalising your opponents

Many players are put off negative doubles because they feel that they preclude the chance to penalize their opponents. They do not. In fact, they really offer your side the opportunity for a more informed penalty double, generated through fuller knowledge of the hand patterns, the fits or lack of them, and the avoidance of making a bad bid, when you could just pass and await developments.

Negative doubles are a true partnership tool, and both members must be aware of their use, especially when trying to penalize the opposition.

Because you can no longer make an immediate penalty double, you will have to pass and wait for your partner to reopen the bidding. This will often be with a take-out double, which you will pass, converting it to penalties. You may miss the occasional golden opportunity, but you will also miss the times when it was wrong for you to double the opposition. In fact, the pros outweigh the cons.

Partner opens 1S, RHO overcalls 2H:

a)   ♠   Q8   b)   ♠   4
     ♡   962   ♡   KJ982
     ◇   K764   ◇   AQ52
     ♣   AQ98   ♣   932

a)   Double – a standard negative double, here showing
     both minors.

b)   Pass. You might bid NTs, but you have a misfit with
     partner and your first thought should be to defend.
     By passing, you allow your partner the chance to
     re-open with a take-out double, which you will pass,
     converting it to penalties.

     If he fails to re-open, it may be that he had opened
     light, and would not have stood a penalty double,
     even if you could have made one immediately. On
     that basis, you are quite well off just defending 2H
     undoubled.

     *This means that, as opener, you are under pressure
     to re-open with double as often as possible. This you
     should do whenever you hold a shortage in the
     opponent's suit, even if you do not hold 3-card
     support for all the remaining suits.*

You should also re-open with double whenever you
hold a very strong hand, regardless of shape.

You open 1S, LHO overcalls 2H, partner and RHO pass:

c)   ♠   AQ752   d)   ♠   A532   e) ♠ KQJ987
     ♡   4   ♡   984   ♡ 543
     ◇   J43   ◇   KJ8   ◇ KJ8
     ♣   AJ84   ♣   AKQ   ♣ Q

c)   Double. You may be minimum, but you are short in
     hearts, and that means that your partner is likely to

hold length in hearts and is waiting to penalize your opposition in 2H.

What else can be happening? You are quite weak, so if partner has nothing the opposition should be bidding on. If partner were short in hearts, the opposition would be barraging; if partner held 3-card spade support or better, he would have supported you; if he held both minors, he would have made a negative double. You virtually *know* that he will pass your re-opening double, and that defending 2H will offer the best chance of a decent plus score.

d) Double. You have the wrong shape for a double, but you are too strong to pass, particularly as it is still possible that partner wants to double your opponents.

Notice the massacre that will occur when you re-open with double on hands c) and d) and your partner holds hand b) opposite. He will pass for penalties, and your opponents will not enjoy themselves.

e) 2S. You are not short in hearts, and your hand is good only for playing with spades as trumps.

So, whenever you hold a shortage in the opponent's suit, your first instinct must be to re-open with a double, particularly if your points are scattered around your hand, and not concentrated in one or two long suits. The fact that your partner has not supported you or made a negative double should reassure you that you have no fit available, and that your side should be defending.

Finally, when the responder passes, and then subsequently doubles, it will be for penalties. A negative double only applies to a double immediately after the first overcall. This is an important understanding, allowing you to be confident in situations like this:

Dealer East   ♠ 85
E/W Vul.   ♡ KJ1098
                  ◊ 6
                  ♣ A10873

N	E	S	W
–	–	1D	1H
NB	2H	NB	NB
Dbl	all pass		

♠ QJ10   **N**   ♠ 7643
♡ AQ653   **W   E**   ♡ 742
◊ KJ94   **S**   ◊ 107
♣ 5   ♣ KQJ2

                  ♠ AK92
                  ♡ –
                  ◊ AQ8532
                  ♣ 964

North's double is definitely for penalties, confirming that his original pass was based on wanting to make a penalty double of West's 1H overcall. Notice that South had to resist bidding 2S or 3D at his second turn. This should be easy once he reflects that either his partner is exceptionally weak or, as he did not make a negative double, he is denying even a 4-card spade suit. As South is void in hearts, there is every chance that North is long in them and will make a penalty double.

Look, also, at South's defensive tricks. If North is short in diamonds and spades – as we expect him to be on the bidding, aces and kings are exactly what we want to take tricks quickly and start a ruffing situation if it is required.

COMPETITIVE DOUBLES

One of the toughest competitive situations is where you open the bidding, LHO passes, partner responds, and RHO intervenes. Frequently, this overcall prevents you from re-bidding your suit at the lowest level or re-bidding NTs because you lack the double stopper which is then required.

Penalty doubles in this situation are only rarely of use. In any case, penalties can still be extracted via a pass by the opener followed by a conversion of a subsequent re-opening double by partner.

Correct understanding of the principles of bidding in this position, together with another use for the most flexible bid in the game – double – can actually turn what is an interference into an extra opportunity for hand description.

Here are the six main situations.

You are West, the opener:

1. W
    ♠ 8
    ♡ AJ7
    ♢ AQJ76
    ♣ 8643

N	E	S	W
–	–	–	1D
NB	1S	2C	?

Pass. You are minimum for your opening bid, and Pass shows that you have no extra values or extra length in your suit. However, Pass does guarantee that your suit contains at least five cards because your hand must be unbalanced. If you held only a 4-card suit, you would either have opened 1NT, rebid NTs now, or doubled (see below).

2. W

	♠	Q3
♡	A4
◊	AQJ976
♣	642

N	E	S	W
–	–	–	1D
NB	1S	2C	?

2D. You are not minimum, and you hold extra length in your suit. Rebidding your minor suit guarantees a 6-card suit as, with only a 5-card suit, you would either pass or show a strong balanced hand by rebidding NTs or doubling (see below).

Rebidding a major suit suggests a 6-card suit, but may be made on a strong unbalanced hand containing only a 5-card major suit of high quality.

3. W

♠	K3
♡	A62
◊	AQJ92
♣	Q42

N	E	S	W
–	–	–	1D
NB	1S	2C	?

Double. This is the toughest type of hand to bid after an intervention by your RHO. Double here means that you hold a hand on which you would have rebid NTs, but you are unable to because you lack the two stoppers in the opponent's suit you now require. Double therefore promises a balanced hand of 15-20 points, with one or no stopper in the opponent's suit. Partner can pass this double – converting it to penalties – if he holds length in the opponent's suit and no fit with your original suit, or he might bid NTs if he holds a stopper in the opponent's suit. Otherwise, he simply continues bidding as if you had rebid 1NT without the intervention.

Notice how wonderfully flexible this action is. It allows you to describe your hand very accurately, letting partner know that your side holds the clear majority of points, and keeping all options open, including penalising your opponents.

This is particularly relevant when the opponents intervene at a high level:

4. W

♠ K9
♡ KQJ4
◇ AQ85
♣ Q54

N	E	S	W
–	–	–	1D
NB	1S	4C	?

Double. This is still only a Double to show that you were planning to rebid at least 1NT, and partner still has the option of bidding on if he holds a distributional hand. However, as it shows a balanced hand – denying 4-card spade support obviously – unless partner's hand contains some very long suits, he will know that it cannot be right to continue bidding at the 4-level or higher. This being so, he will pass your double for penalties.

5. W

♠ K3
♡ A76
◇ AJ964
♣ AQ5

N	E	S	W
–	–	–	1D
NB	1S	2C	?

2NT. You were planning to rebid NTs and, with two stoppers in the opponent's suit, there is no need to alter your plan. The range of your 2NT rebid in this situation is slightly wider than usual, encompassing all but the worst 15 point hands, up to 18 points. The excellent position of your club honours should compensate for any shortfall in high card values.

6. W

♠ K3
♡ A764
◇ AJ96
♣ AQ5

N	E	S	W
–	–	–	1D
NB	1S	Dbl	?

Redouble. Over South's take-out double, Redouble confirms that you were planning to rebid NTs, and that your side holds the clear majority of points. The prime reason to Redouble is to suggest a penalty of your opponent's contract and, for that reason, you are likely to be short in partner's suit, even to the extent of holding a singleton with a 5-4-3-1 shape of hand. Any subsequent doubles by either you or your partner will be for penalties.

Opposite a 1-level response from partner, you require 16+ points – ensuring that you do hold the clear balance of points; opposite a 2-level response from partner, 15 points will suffice.

All these sequences are based on a specific auction where LHO passes, partner changes the suit, and RHO intervenes.

If partner raises your suit or passes, double has different meanings.

If partner passes your opening bid:

W

♠ KQ9
♡ KQJ7
◇ AK964
♣ 5

N	E	S	W
–	–	–	1D
NB	NB	2C	?

Double. This is for take-out, suggesting a hand at the top end of the opening points range, and promising at least 3-card support for each of the unbid suits.

W

♠ AQ8
♡ J74
◇ AKQ64
♣ K6

N	E	S	W
–	–	–	1D
NB	NB	1S	?

1NT. As partner has not responded and therefore presumably holds fewer than 6 points, the 1NT rebid now shows 19-20 points with two stoppers in the opponent's suit (or slightly fewer with a long suit and one stopper in the overcalled suit).

You would be most reluctant to rebid 2NT over a 2-level overcall, unless your hand contained at least a 5-card suit with a definite source of tricks.

If partner raises your suit, you enter territory where it is vital to distinguish between merely wanting to compete the part-score, and still wishing to make a try for game. The usual precepts of new suits being forcing are applicable here, along with a further use of Double as a competitive tool.

W

♠ 83
♡ AQJ76
◇ 96
♣ KQJ5

N	E	S	W
–	–	–	1H
NB	2H	3D	?

3H. Here, you simply wish to compete to 3H as you believe that you hold nine trumps between you, and you do not want your partner to bid 4H even if he was maximum for his 2H raise. *Continuing to bid your own suit in a competitive auction is never invitational.*

W

♠ AQJ76
♡ KQ85
◇ 95
♣ K3

N	E	S	W
–	–	–	1S
NB	2S	3D	?

3H. If there is room to introduce a new suit below the level of your own agreed suit, this is a clear game try. This new suit need not necessarily be a 4-card suit, but it should contain some decent values. What the introduction of a new suit does promise is that your original suit contains at least five cards, and that your hand contains extra high card points.

If partner is minimum for his 2S raise, he returns to 3S; if maximum, to 4S. Unless you agree otherwise, this new suit should not be played as a weak suit Trial Bid after the opponents intervene.

W

♠ K3
♡ AQJ76
◇ 96
♣ KQ85

N	E	S	W
–	–	–	1H
NB	2H	3D	?

Double. Here, there is no room to introduce your new suit at a level which would allow you to sign off below game if partner does not wish to accept your game try. As you have agreed a suit, Double should not be taken as penalties but as a game try manoeuvre. If the responder was minimum for his raise, he can still sign off in 3H; if he was maximum he can bid 4H immediately.

This is the same in situations where both opponents are competing:

W

♠ 83
♡ AKJ7
◇ KQ42
♣ KQ8

N	E	S	W
–	–	–	1H
1S	2H	2S	?

Double. You want to make a try for game, but you cannot rebid 3D as this would guarantee a 5-card heart suit. Double in this situation does not deny a 5-card suit, but it is often indicative of a reasonably balanced hand, and partner should be aware that you may be making a game try on the basis of a very strong opening hand with only a 4-card suit.

If partner is maximum for his raise, he goes to game; if he was minimum, or if he raised with only 3-card support, he signs off in 3H.

In all these game try situations when you double, partner has the option of passing, converting it to penalties.

This is particularly true when you have both bid and agreed a suit, as in the example above.

Then if your partner makes a game try double on a hand where his suit may only be four cards, you should consider passing with a maximum raise, including only 3-card support.

W

♠ 982
♡ J987
◇ 64
♣ AK85

N	E	S	W
–	1S	2H	2S
3H	Dbl	NB	?

Pass. You correctly raised partner's 1S to 2S but, now, you have the opportunity of converting your partner's game try double to penalties. Even if partner does hold a 5-card spade suit, your hand is not particularly suitable for game whereas, considering that you made only a simple raise on the first round of the auction, you hold excellent defensive values. Also, you hold only 3-card spade support, meaning that you are short of trump length to bid on.

Penalty Double

Before we leave competitive doubling, there is one last situation which demands a little attention. That is the Penalty Double.

W

♠ AJ5
♡ K104
◇ Q9643
♣ AK

N	E	S	W
–	–	1NT	?

Double. After all these take-out and value-showing doubles, you will be delighted to discover that the penalty double does still exist. I strongly recommend that you play all doubles of 1NT as mandatory penalty doubles – that is to say, partner cannot remove the double, however weak he may be.

This does mean that 1NT doubled will make occasionally and that you will have to be fully up to strength to make the penalty double – I recommend the equivalent of 17 points (i.e. 16 points with good intermediates or a 5-card suit).

However, it also means that when you double 1NT on a delicious 20-count, you will not have to face a miserable partner who bids at the 2-level on a 4-card suit, just because he thinks he can't stand your double.

It also means that partner will pass when you double on this type of hand:

W		N	E	S	W
♠ 932		–	–	1NT	?
♡ A54					
◇ AKQ964					
♣ 5					

Double. You are on lead, and you should be hopeful of the first seven tricks. If partner hasn't told you what you should lead at trick 8 by then, your signalling system is not up to much.

You should double on this hand even if your suit were hearts or spades because, if partner holds nothing, you will still record a plus score defending 1NT doubled, and you couldn't make 2-of-a-suit. If partner does hold tricks for you, so that you can make a 2 or 3 or 4-level contract, then you will be defeating 1NT doubled by even more. In fact, you will almost always get richer doubling 1NT with a long suit than by bidding it.

Should the opponents wriggle out of the double, you can always bid your suit later, indicating a strong hand with a long suit – a better description than an immediate overcall.

How to get out of 1NT if your opponents double
Now, we must move to the other side of the table, to discuss how we deal with penalty doubles of 1NT. Some people play complicated transfer or relay sequences here, but the natural method often works well, especially against inexperienced opponents.

W

♠ 932
♡ 5432
◇ 9643
♣ 52

N	E	S	W
–		1NT	Dbl	?

2D. Don't just sit there, bid something! Clearly, you are booked for a very large minus score, but if you bid quickly and confidently, your opponents may settle for their game rather than penalising you. In fact, most pairs would have no understanding what double would mean after this sequence. One player may be certain that it is a penalty double; his partner may be equally convinced that it is for take-out. The important element from your point of view is that to pass is to offer your opponents a certain huge score; to bid gives them many opportunities to misjudge the situation.

W

♠ K107
♡ 954
◇ Q964
♣ Q105

N	E	S	W
–		1NT	Dbl	?

Pass. You cannot think of a better spot than 1NT for your side. Notice that pass suggests a balanced hand with some points as, with none, you would have bid something.

W

♠ QJ986
♡ 54
◇ K64
♣ Q102

N	E	S	W
–		1NT	Dbl	?

2S. 1NT may make, but there is a danger that East has doubled holding a long solid heart suit, and he may be able to rattle off seven or eight tricks before your side gains the lead. 2S then is safer.

W				
	N	E	S	W
♠ K109	–		1NT	Dbl	?
♡ A54				
◊ Q1053				
♣ Q42				

Redouble. This is the sort of hand which makes you glad you are playing natural methods, so that you can punish the unlucky or, more likely, rash, doublers of 1NT. Redouble is for business – either you are going to make 1NT redoubled, which is game, or you are going to double whatever the opponents try to slink off into.

As usual Redouble confirms that your side holds the clear majority of points, and that you want to penalize the opposition.

I recommend 10 points or more for Redouble in this position, but I am fairly cautious when it comes to bidding over 1NT. If you want to live life on the edge, you may choose to Redouble with a classy 8 points or more.

1NT OPENER'S
CONSULTATIVE REDOUBLE

There is one further use of Redouble in this type of auction which has a different, and quite powerful, meaning:

W

♠ K32
♡ 54
◇ KQ964
♣ A85

N	E	S	W
–	–	–	1NT
Dbl	NB	NB	?

This is a typical problem for a 1NT opener who has been doubled. Partner has passed over the penalty double, so is marked with some points and a flat hand. Should you pass now, or rescue yourself into 2D?

One solution is to play Redouble in this situation to mean that you have a 5-card suit which you are thinking about bidding, and you want to consult your partner. If he is happy to play in 1NT redoubled, because he is holding 7-9 points, he may pass, and you will be going for the big one, or you may frighten the opposition into bidding themselves. If partner likes the idea of you bidding your 5-card suit – when he is 4-3-3-3 and 4-6 points – he can bid 2C, and you then pass if clubs are your suit, or bid your 5-card suit at the 2-level.

Not only does this gadget bring partner into this delicate decision, but it also provides an opportunity to catch the opposition out when you hold the majority of points and decide to go for 1NT redoubled. It is aggressive, and you may come a cropper occasionally but, in the long run, you will find it beneficial.

RE-OPENING AFTER OPENING 1NT

This is a still more aggressive move, best reserved for the duplicate table. It is clearest in example form:

W	N	E	S	W
♠ QJ98	–	–	–	1NT
♡ 82	2H	NB	NB	Dbl
◇ AQ109				
♣ KJ8				

Once again, you may assume that the points are balanced between the two partnerships and, it seems likely from your hand, your opponents may well have found their 8-card fit. On that assumption, it will be right to compete further. If they do hold an 8-card heart fit, then you hold an 8-card fit somewhere and you hold excellent support for each suit; if they do not, then your partner will hold four hearts and may convert your take-out double to penalties on the TTP.

To re-open with a take-out double having opened 1NT, you require a small doubleton in the suit overcalled (so that all your values are concentrated in the other suits), good texture in the remaining suits and, when the opponent has overcalled a major suit, 4-card support for the other major. Does this mean that you cannot re-open without 4-card support for the other major? It all depends on how aggressive you feel.

In response, if you hold more than one 4-card suit, and you do not know which to bid first, you may require a "scramble" to locate your 8-card fit safely.

Scramble

When your partner has opened 1NT and re-opens with a take-out double, you may be faced with an unpalatable choice.

W

♠ A32
♡ 54
◇ J986
♣ Q432

N	E	S	W
–	1NT	2S	NB
NB	Dbl	NB	?

You should not be too dismayed by this development because you know that your opponents do hold eight spades between them (partner's re-opening double promises a small doubleton in the opponent's suit). However, it is your duty to guide your side into the safest contract available. As partner holds 4-card heart support (he most probably promised 4-card support for the other major), he is presumably 4-3 in the minors. Your duty is to guess which one of your two suits to bid.

The good news is that you do not have to guess. A bid of **2NT** cannot be natural, as you would either have bid it on the first round of bidding, or be passing 2S doubled for penalties if you held good spades. Therefore a bid of 2NT in this situation is played as a scramble. It tells your partner that you have two possible suits to bid, and you want him to bid his suits in ascending order until you find your 4-4 fit. It works like this:

Dealer N   ♠ 63
Love All   ♡ KQ109
         ♢ Q53
         ♣ AQ108

N	E	S	W
1NT	2S	NB	NB
Dbl	NB	2NT	NB
3C	all pass		

♠ Q4   ♠ AK10875
♡ 8653   ♡ A72
♢ A982   ♢ 107
♣ J52   ♣ 73

        ♠ J92
        ♡ J4
        ♢ KJ64
        ♣ K964

North reopens with a double, and South scrambles by bidding 2NT, telling partner that he has two possible places to play. North now rebids his 4-card suits in ascending order (in this sequence he can only hold one 4-card minor suit, as his other 4-card suit is the other major – hearts). The 4-4 fit is found, and 3C just makes whilst, if East pushes on to 3S, he will be defeated.

Notice that playing in the 4-3 fit in 3D will not succeed.

FOURTH SUIT FORCING

I hope that everyone plays Fourth Suit Forcing, because it really is a basic part of the system. As well as being useful simply as a forcing "noise" to make partner bid again, its use accurately indicates your holding in the fourth suit.

Here is the basic situation:

N	E	S	W
–	1H	NB	1S
NB	2C	NB	?

If you, as West, now bid NTs, you are promising two stoppers in the unbid suit – diamonds.

If you bid 2D – Fourth Suit Forcing – you are suggesting one stopper in diamonds. You can confirm a NT hand with one solid stopper by subsequently bidding NTs.

You may use Fourth Suit Forcing without a stopper in the fourth suit when you are looking for a possible slam, or even when you want to play in 3NT with a long solid suit, and need just one stopper from partner to make the game a good bet.

Some players play Fourth Suit Forcing as unconditionally forcing to game but it is probably more flexible to agree that the opener must continue bidding until game is reached whereas responder (the instigator of 4SF) may occasionally pass below game if a misfit becomes apparent.

In terms of point-count, to use Fourth Suit Forcing at the 1 and 2-levels, you require a minimum of 11 points. At the 3-level, you should have sufficient values to sustain that game contract. There is no upper limit. Indeed, Fourth Suit Forcing is sometimes used to identify a good fit as a prelude to a slam try.

Before moving on to the responses to Fourth Suit Forcing, which is where problems usually occur, let's take a quick look at one important sequence.

W

	N	E	S	W
♠ K32				
♡ AQJ54	–	–	–	1H
◇ Q986				
♣ 2	NB	1S	NB	?

There is only one sensible rebid here, and that is 2S. If partner is weak, this is likely to be the best part-score; if he is strong, he will only insist on spades with a 5-card suit or better. Even a 4-3 fit will play adequately, because your singleton club can be utilised for ruffing.

5-4-3-1 hands are very strong when you can support partner's suit with your 3 or 4-card suit, but much weaker if you end up in your own suit or in NTs.

Rebids after partner has used Fourth Suit Forcing

With that out of the way, we can proceed to our rebids after partner has used Fourth Suit Forcing. The following examples show the most effective useful ways to rebid, where you can maximise your score or control a misfit situation with constructive damage limitation. In each case you are West and the bidding has followed the same pattern:

1. With a stopper in the fourth suit, rebid NT:

W

♠ 32
♡ AQJ54
◊ Q6
♣ KJ98

N	E	S	W
–	–	–	1H
NB	1S	NB	2C
NB	2D	NB	2NT

As partner has used Fourth Suit Forcing you can assume that he holds one stopper in diamonds, and this makes your ◊Qx a minimum help in the fourth suit, but very suitable, particularly when partner holds ◊Kxx or ◊Axx. Now, with the lead coming around to you, you have two stoppers in the suit.

As partner has promised 11 points or more when using Fourth Suit Forcing, if you hold a good 14 points or more, you should rebid 3NT immediately.

2. With extra distribution, bid out your shape. With a fifth card in your second suit, you should rebid that suit to show 5-5 shape.

W

♠ 2
♡ AKJ98
◊ 86
♣ AJ852

N	E	S	W
–	–	–	1H
NB	1S	NB	2C
NB	2D	NB	3C

3. And with a sixth card in your first suit (unless you are completely minimum, when you might just rebid your original suit) you should make a jump rebid in that suit to show 6-4 shape:

W

♠ 2
♡ KQ7654
◊ 83
♣ AK85

N	E	S	W
–	–	–	1H
NB	1S	NB	2C
NB	2D	NB	3H

When your partner responds initially with a major suit, if you hold 3-card support and a weak hand (either 11-14 points or 7 losers, depending upon how you value your hand), you will have supported him last time.

4. With a stronger hand, you should now jump to show your 5-4-3-1 shape and non-minimum hand:

W

♠ K64
♡ AKJ98
◊ 2
♣ AJ94

N	E	S	W
–	–	–	1H
NB	1S	NB	2C
NB	2D	NB	3S

5. This, in turn, permits you to show good 2-card support for the major suit by supporting partner's suit at the lowest available level. This enables you to stop in the 5-2 major-suit fit when this is the least awful part-score.

W

♠ A2
♡ AJ532
◊ 53
♣ A964

N	E	S	W
–	–	–	1H
NB	1S	NB	2C
NB	2D	NB	2S

If partner's first response is a minor suit, you will support him, after Fourth Suit Forcing, at the minimum level with 3-card support and a 5-4-3-1 hand. You would never support a minor suit with only 2-card support.

6. If your hand fits none of the above, the best you can do is to rebid your first suit at the lowest available level. This will show a hand unable even to show doubleton support for partner's major suit, and without a stopper in the fourth suit. Indeed, it is shouting loudly that the hand is a horrible misfit:

W

♠ 2
♡ AKJ74
♢ 954
♣ KQ96

N	E	S	W
–	–	–	1H
NB	1S	NB	2C
NB	2D	NB	2H

STRENGTHENING YOUR SYSTEM:
KEY POINTS TO REMEMBER

Each of the elements contained in this system is self-sufficient, as I said at the beginning of the section, and you can choose to add any one or combination of these conventions to your system. I certainly recommend working through the list slowly with your partner or group of friends, introducing the gadgets slowly.

The important factor to remember is that not only must you learn the new material, but you must also concentrate on the new sets of positive and negative inferences that can then be taken. For example:

N	E	S	W
–	NB	1D	NB
1S	2H		

Your partner, East, deals and passes. Subsequently, he enters the bidding with a 2-level overcall. Normally, you would assume that this would show a 6-card suit but, if you are playing Weak 2s, it cannot be, or he would have opened 2H, or 1H, originally.

As you introduce Weak 2s, Negative and Competitive doubles into your system, you will find that your style becomes still more aggressive. Be prepared for some poor results, especially while you are still learning the details of your system. Also, try to remember that no system works well all the time. Some sets of hands will suit the system, others will not. But, if you play these additions to your system well, you will be playing enough to ensure that, with decent card-play and defence, you can score upwards of 60% whenever you play. That will put you in the top quarter of each competition, or make you a healthy, wealthy winner of your rubber bridge or Chicago afternoons.

When you play duplicate pairs, or teams of four, both members of your partnership should have an identically completed convention card. If you were to introduce all the elements of Part 3, this is how your card would look. If you disagree with any element, simply replace it with your chosen methods.

Basic System – Acol, with major-suit Weak Twos

OPENING BIDS	Point Range	Min. length	CONVENTIONAL MEANING	SPECIAL RESPONSES
1♣	10+	4	Natural	} Splinters; 3NT "pudding raise"
1◊	10+	4	Natural	} 4-card support 12-15pts
1♡	11+	4	Natural	} Splinters; 3NT = "pudding raise"
1♠	11+	4	Natural	} 4-card support 12-15pts
1NT	12-14	-		Stayman; Transfers
2♣	-	-	Game Force	2◊ = relay; 2♡ = double negative
2◊	-	-	Strong 1-suiter, with 8-9½ playing tricks	2♡ = relay
2♡	5-9	5/6	Weak	2NT = forcing enquiry; bids non-forcing
2♠	5-9	5/6	Weak	2NT = forcing enquiry; bids non-forcing
2NT	21-22	-	Natural	Modified Baron; Transfers
3 bids	5-9	7	Pre-empt; 1st/2nd: good suit	
4 bids	5-13	7	Natural	

DEFENSIVE BIDS				
OVER-CALLS	Meaning		OPPONENTS OPEN	Defensive Methods
Simple	5-card suit; 7-17pts		Strong 1♣	Weak J.O
Jump	Weak; 4th = strong		Weak 1NT	} insert your chosen conventional defence
Cue-bid	Michaers		Strong 1NT	} here, or write "natural"
1NT	Direct=16-18pts; 4th=10-14pts		Weak 2 Bids	2NT=16-19pts; Dbl:T.O; Lebensohl
responses	Stayman; Transfers		Weak 3 Bids	Dbl = T.O
2NT	Direct=Unusual; 4th=19-21pts		4 Bids	Dbl = values; 4NT = T.O
responses	4th=Modified Baron; Transfers		Multi	insert your chosen defence here

ACTION AFTER OPPONENTS INTERVENE WITH	
Simple Overcall	Double: Sputnik — Bids: Forcing
Jump Overcall	Double: Sputnik — Bids: Forcing
Double	Redouble;10+ New Suit: Forcing Jump in New Suit: Fit Jump
	Jump Raise: Barrage 2NT: Strong Raise

PART FOUR
SLAM BIDDING

ALTHOUGH slam contracts, whether missed or made, tend to stick in the mind, bridge competitions, be they rubber, teams or duplicate, are rarely won and lost on the basis of slams. However, there is little more satisfying than uncovering a slim small slam, or nailing the grand. If you can smile across the table at your partner before each hand, because you both feel confident, your bridge will be better and more enjoyable and, importantly, it should be just the opposite for your opposition. This is not some vague, ethereal theory, this is fact, and it will show itself as higher percentages and bigger winnings.

Almost all experts use Splinters, Cue-bidding, and Roman Key Card Blackwood, and these are the conventions we will be discussing here. For regular partnerships or groups, there are two further understandings which can prove useful: Quantitative Bids and Exclusion Blackwood. In each case, the skill is not in remembering how these gadgets work, rather it is choosing the right moment to apply each, and interpreting the information accordingly. Whilst I have no desire to dissuade you from bidding slam contracts, I think that the right attitude to these conventions is that they are at your disposal to prevent you from reaching bad slams, more than rocketing you to the 6 or 7-level.

Points are not that important for slams. Hand distribution, sources of tricks, and controls in each suit are what count, and these you must discover from the preceding auction. In the same way that your fit with partner, both in length and the position of your high cards is important in competitive bidding, so it is here.

For this reason, Splinters fit in very well with our system and the simple methods that I suggest here are easy to learn and adopt, and will add a powerful weapon to your artillery.

Roman Key Card Blackwood, Cue-bidding and Exclusion Blackwood are precise tools for reaching slam contracts, once you have established a good fit and sufficient values. Quantitative bidding is vital when your target is a No-trump slam, and you are merely interested in whether partner is minimum or maximum for his bidding up to that point.

SPLINTERS

When you open the bidding at the 1-level (or respond at the 1 or 2-level) and receive support from partner, two key factors will decide whether a slam is worth contemplating:

- Firstly, do the partnership's two hands contain sufficient distribution, in terms of ruffing values and suits, to make twelve or thirteen tricks possible?

- Secondly, do you have controls (aces and kings) in all four suits, to avoid losing quick tricks?

The shape of partner's hand – the one that will be dummy – is vital. Without good distribution, a limit raise opposite a 1-level opener (or simple response) will not be good enough to make a slam-try worth the risks involved. To this end, "Splinter Bids" were invented, which show immediately whether responder's hand contains a singleton or void, as well as 4-card support for the opener's suit. If the ruffing value shown corresponds with the weakness in opener's hand, that may be impetus enough to instigate slam enquiries.

It is implicit in good bridge that, if you hold 4-card support for your partner's major suit, you must show this immediately. Playing our simple Splinters allows you to show this feature with all point-counts from 5 points upwards. If you do not support your partner's major suit immediately, you are denying 4-card support.

This is how our supporting chart will look now (you may prefer to make the Losing Trick Count your guide to limit raises):

1H - 2H	5-9 points
1H - 3H	10-12 points
1H - 4H	less than 10 points, with extra good distribution
1H - 3NT	**12-15 points, 4-card support, no singleton or void**
1H - SPLINTER	**10-14 points, 4-card support, singleton, or void, in the suit bid**
1H - Jump shift	showing either excellent support or self-supporting suit of your own with definite slam intentions.

Notice that the only new bids are the 3NT response and the Splinter itself – everything else stays the same.

The Pudding Raise

The 3NT response shown above, which we call a "Pudding Raise", replaces the inefficient and outmoded Delayed Game Raise. Although it is not forcing, as you are showing 4-card support or more for partner's major, he will almost always correct back to the trump contract.

With a minor suit fit, the pudding raise of 3NT still shows 4-card support with 12-15 points, but denies a 4-card major suit which could have been responded at the 1-level. Unless he has slam aspirations, the opener usually passes the 3NT response as, with a minor suit fit, it is likely to be the best contract.

Examples:

a)

W	E		
♠ AK853	♠ Q974	**W**	**E**
♡ AQ63	♡ K5	1S	3NT
◇ 43	◇ Q85	4S	
♣ 42	♣ AQ65		

a) A simple replacement for the Delayed Game Raise, the pudding raise shows 4-card spade support, no singleton or void, and 12-15 points. Partner settles for the safe major suit game.

b)

W	E
♠ K98	♠ Q63
♡ A43	♡ K5
◊ AQJ76	◊ K532
♣ J5	♣ AQ63

W	E
1D	3NT
NB	

b) 3NT has the same meaning opposite a minor suit opening but here, the opener passes the response and plays in the sensible game contract.

Following the pudding raise, a bid in a new suit is a cue-bid and a slam try; 4NT is Blackwood.

c)

W	E
♠ AQ853	♠ K974
♡ AQJ9	♡ K5
◊ 93	◊ AK5
♣ A2	♣ 9753

W	E
1S	3NT
4C	4D
6S	

c) Following the pudding raise, West wants to investigate for a slam. Worried about two quick diamond losers, he cue-bids 4C to show ♣A; East shows his ◊A, and that is enough for West to have a go at 6S.

East cannot hold ◊A and all four kings, as he would be strong enough to jump-shift. Indeed, with a little more distribution, he would be jump-shifting or making a splinter – the pudding raise indicates a *flat* hand with 12-15 points.

The pudding raise is, however, merely a useful by-product of Splinters.

Splinter Bids

Any double jump in response to an opening 1-level bid is now a Splinter, which shows at least 4-card support for opener's suit, a singleton (or void) in the suit bid, and enough points to make game a good bet opposite a fairly minimum opening hand.

To make a splinter with fewer than about 10 points is likely to lead to trouble, so this should be your lower limit. There need be no upper limit however as, if partner signs off after your splinter, you can always start up the bidding again with a cue-bid if you still feel slam is a good chance opposite a minimum opener.

If you make this agreement with partner, you can then add the important inference that when partner makes a jump-shift and subsequently supports your suit, you will know that his hand cannot also contain a singleton, as he would have preferred a splinter to the jump-shift in the first instance.

Partner opens 1H:

a)	b)	c)	d)
♠ 3	♠ 97542	♠ A54	♠ J76
♡ KQ43	♡ KQ98	♡ Q965	♡ K832
◇ AJ432	◇ AJ53	◇ 8	◇ AK5
♣ A98	♣ –	♣ KQ854	♣ K64

a) Respond 3S. This can never be a natural bid. If you had a strong suit of spades, you would respond 1S first, and then keep bidding them. This is a splinter, showing a singleton spade, 4-card heart support or better, and a desire to play at the game level or higher.

b)   Respond 4C. Again a splinter. Despite only holding 10 points, your hand is worth a raise to 4H and, if partner holds his values in your three suits, a slam may be possible.

c)   Respond 4D. A classic splinter.

d)   Respond 3NT. No singleton or void, so a pudding raise is correct.

The real beauty of Splinters is that they immediately focus partner's attention on the working elements of his hand, allowing him to judge whether a slam is a reasonable prospect.

W	E		W	E
♠ KQ986	♠ A532		1S	4C
♡ AK72	♡ J543		?	
◇ 3	◇ AK85			
♣ A98	♣ 5			

West holds only a modest 16 points but, all of a sudden, his hand has grown in stature enormously. The 4-card spade support makes his trump suit very robust, and East's singleton club opposite his ace means that he has no club losers to worry about. He has a source of tricks both from club ruffs and from his heart suit. A quick check that he is not missing two aces, and he can bid 6S without too many worries.

W	E		W	E
♠ KQ5	♠ 3		1H	3S
♡ AK984	♡ QJ52		?	
◇ KJ7	◇ AQ852			
♣ 53	♣ K97			

Here, life is not so rosy. There might still be a slam if East
has plenty of aces, but, crucially, West's spade holding
opposite East's singleton or void is now waste-paper, and
he does not appear to have any other marked source of
tricks. This, together with missing three aces, should
persuade him to settle for a quiet 4H.

W	E
♠ A9853	♠ KQJ4
♡ AJ4	♡ 972
◇ KJ3	◇ AQ1098
♣ 92	♣ A

W	E
1S	4C
4S	5D
5H	6C
6D	7S

West is not particularly enamoured of East's singleton
club and, with a minimum hand, correctly signs off in
game. However, when East shows a very strong hand by
bidding on, cue-bidding 5D, West should realise that his
hand contains some very good features: no wasted points
in clubs; excellent diamonds and hearts. He cue-bids his
♡A, East cue-bids 6C, showing a club void or singleton
♣A. West now shows ◇K and, all of a sudden the grand
slam is reached. Even reaching 6S would have been a
pretty good result.

Splinters can also be played as an opener's rebid, in
sequences such as these:

W	E
1H	1S
4C	

W	E
1C	1H
3S	

W	E
1S	2C
4D	

Notice that in each case, the opener bids at *the third available level* – this is the simple way to agree to play Splinters,
which will avoid any possible confusion.

In case you are worried that you may forget that these
bids are Splinters, just remember the simple rule that:

> *any bid which is made at a level higher than would
> have been natural and forcing must agree the last bid
> suit.*

Then, it is up to you and your partner to agree that such
a bid will be a Splinter, or any other gadget you fancy.

Once your partner has splintered, you can sign off by
returning to the agreed suit at game level, or introduce a
new suit as a cue-bid and slam try, or Blackwood. The
most important understanding is that the Splinter agrees
the last suit bid and, when launching into Blackwood or
cue-bidding, that is the relevant trump suit.

ROMAN KEY CARD
BLACKWOOD

Virtually every expert pair in the world plays Roman Key Card Blackwood, or a variation on the theme, because it is, unquestionably, a substantial improvement on ordinary Blackwood.

Roman Key Card Blackwood provides an ace-count as in standard Blackwood, but it also concentrates on the quality of the trump suit, which is always vital at slam level, and particularly so for grand slams. The king of trumps is counted as a fifth "ace", and the convention shows the queen of trumps as well. Once all this information has been sent and received, there is time to cue-bid kings. When hunting for that elusive grand slam, you are interested in precisely which kings your partner holds, and Roman Key Card Blackwood allows you to find that information.

Because Roman Key Card Blackwood is so comprehensive, you can delete the grand slam force from your card, for all but the rarest of situations.

Once the trump suit has been agreed, 4NT asks for the number of aces in partner's hand. The innovation is that there are now **five** "aces" – the king of trumps being the fifth ace. The responses are:

5C	=	0 or 3 aces
5D	=	1 or 4 aces
5H	=	2 aces; no queen of trumps
5S	=	2 aces; with queen of trumps

You will have no difficulty deciphering whether partner holds the upper or lower count of aces after the 5C or 5D

responses. If you can't fathom out the difference between
three aces in your partner's hand, you obviously have not
done enough bidding before wading in with Roman Key
Card Blackwood.

Asking for the trump queen

Following the 5C or 5D response, you may enquire
whether partner holds the queen of trumps by bidding the
next suit up. If the next suit is the agreed trump suit, you
must bid the next suit above that.

- If partner *does not* hold the queen of trumps, he
  returns to the agreed suit at the lowest available level.

- If partner *does* hold the queen of trumps, he shows a
  useful feature, like a king, or a source of tricks in a suit
  partner has previously bid.

a)

		W	E
W	**E**	2D	2H
♠ AK9832	♠ Q104	2S	3S
♡ KQJ10	♡ A63	4NT	5D
◇ A2	◇ K5	5H	6D
♣ A	♣ 76532	7S/7NT	

a) Using 2D to show a Strong 2, East-West agree
spades, and East's response to Roman Key Card
Blackwood shows his one ace. Now looking for the
grand slam, West enquires about the queen of trumps
by bidding the next suit up from the Roman Key
Card Blackwood response. Without the trump queen,
East would bid 5S (the agreed suit) but, as he holds it,
he bids 6D which not only confirms ♠Q but also

shows a previously unshown extra value – almost always a king.

West can now count thirteen tricks and can bid the grand slam with confidence.

Asking for kings

Having used 4NT, 5NT remains an enquiry for kings, but requires you to *cue-bid* your kings in ascending order. If you hold no kings (other than the king of trumps which you will already have indicated), you should return to the agreed suit.

b)

W	E		W	E
♠ AKJ98	♠ Q432		1S	3S
♡ KQJ43	♡ A5		4NT	5S
◇ A2	◇ 853		7S	
♣ 8	♣ A763			

b) Following East's limit raise, West uses Roman Key Card Blackwood. East's 5S response shows two aces and queen of trumps. As East cannot hold another king for his bid, there is no point asking for kings. However, West can count 12 top tricks and, with a 5-card second suit, the chance of making 13 tricks must be very high, so he should bid 7S.

c)

W	E		W	E
♠ AQ76	♠ K54		1H	3H
♡ AQ75432	♡ K986		4NT	5H
◇ 8	◇ AJ94		5NT	6S
♣ A	♣ 32		7H	

c) West's hand improves dramatically when East supports hearts. East's 5H response to Roman Key Card Blackwood shows two "aces" and no trump queen. As West holds three aces, he knows that East is showing ◊A and the king of trumps. Deciding that if East holds ♠K the grand slam will be a good proposition, West asks East to name his king if he has one. Had East held no kings – other than the trump king which he has already shown – he would return to the agreed suit. As it is, he shows his ♠K by bidding 6S and West proceeds to the grand slam.

    Notice that if West had not wanted to hear about ♠K, he would now be past his safe contract of 6H. If you ask your partner to name his king, you must be able to cope with whichever king you are shown. If it is too risky, settle for the safe small slam.

Often, when you ask for the trump queen, if your partner holds it, he can show you the vital king in his response. This saves you from having to go through the 5NT enquiry.

d)

W	E
♠ KJ843	♠ AQ96
♡ KQJ73	♡ A2
◊ A	◊ 653
♣ 92	♣ AK86

W	E
1S	3C
3H	3S
4NT	5C
5D	6C
7NT	

d) East makes a jump shift to 3C – promising ♣A or ♣K at the head of the suit – and then agrees spades as trumps. Roman Key Card Blackwood then locates every vital card for the Grand Slam.

> East's   5C showed 0 or 3 "aces", which must, on the bidding, be 3.
>
> West's   5D asked for the trump queen.
>
> East's   6C showed the trump queen (5S, the agreed suit, would have denied it), and a feature in clubs, which must be the ♣K.

West would have had to ask for ♣K if he wanted to bid the grand slam, but East could show his immediately with his trump queen confirmation. West could now count 13 tricks, and can bid the grand slam with one hundred per cent confidence. Using ordinary Blackwood, it would be virtually impossible to discover both ♣K and ♠Q.

e)

W	E
♠ A2	♠ KQJ8
♡ A6543	♡ Q972
◇ AKQJ5	◇ 82
♣ 8	♣ K63

W	E
1H	3H
4NT	5C
5H	

e)   As mentioned earlier, the *raison d'être* of slam conventions is to keep you out of bad slams, rather than propelling you into good ones. Here Roman Key Card Blackwood identifies that East's limit raise contains neither ♣A nor the king of trumps. As far as West is concerned, slam can only be on a finesse, at best, and so he signs off. Without Roman Key Card Blackwood, there would be many who would just launch from 3H to 6H. Not a terrible bid, but unnecessary when you have the means of checking for trump honours as well as aces.

f) **W**   **E**

		W	E
♠ AK43	♠ Q98652	1NT	2H
♡ A73	♡ KQ	3D	4NT
◇ 87	◇ AK53	5C	6S
♣ Q972	♣ 6		

f) Here, East is encouraged to slam by West's break of
    the transfer, showing 4-card trump support, a double-
    ton diamond and the right type of hand for a suit
    contract. Again, the trump suit is a worry but, when
    West shows three "aces", East doesn't care which they
    are, 6S must be a good spot.

    Without Roman Key Card Blackwood perhaps East
    would have bid 5S, asking for trump quality.
    However, this fails to find out whether there are two
    missing aces outside the trump suit. Roman Key Card
    Blackwood takes care of that too.

Voids

There are many different ways of dealing with voids, and
they are all singularly unsatisfactory. Thankfully, situations where there is a void are very rare indeed. Hands
containing voids should never institute Roman Key Card
Blackwood (or ordinary Blackwood either), but should, in
the first instance, begin a cue-bidding sequence to locate
precise key cards. It is quite acceptable to start to cue-bid,
and then switch to Roman Key Card Blackwood
subsequently.

When responding to Roman Key Card Blackwood with
a hand containing a void, you should continue to ignore
the void if it was partner's first bid suit.

However, if you feel that it is a void that will be of
benefit to your side's slam chances, in response to the
RKCB 4NT enquiry:

- 5NT shows an *even* number of "aces" plus the working void,

- 6C shows an *odd* number of "aces" plus the working void.

To ask for the queen of trumps, bid the next suit up (or the next if the immediate suit is trumps) and partner will respond as before.

Intervention

In the unlikely event of an intervening bid over 4NT, **DOPI** responses should swing into action. Continue to include the trump king as an ace.

DOPI stands for:
Double = 0 or 3 aces
Pass   = 1 or 4 aces

However, if you are playing against a pair who manage to intervene at this point without your being able to penalise them, and they do it more than once, you may be out of your league!

CUE-BIDDING

Many potential slams are best investigated with a cue-bidding sequence. Sometimes you will glean enough information to choose your slam from cue-bids alone; other times, you may cue-bid and then launch into Roman Key Card Blackwood (or ordinary Blackwood).

The advantages of cue-bidding are many, not least that the level of the auction is kept down, allowing you to sniff out the possibility of a slam without committing yourself to too high a level. However, the real point of cue-bids is that, unlike any form of Blackwood which merely asks partner questions, they both inform partner about your hand and ask him to describe his hand further. In this way, you are bringing your partner into the decision making process.

Also, Blackwood only discovers *how many* aces partner holds, whereas cue-bids can find out *which* controls partner's hand contains.

Cue-bids only occur when a suit has been agreed in a strong sequence, and you are interested in investigating a slam. A cue-bid is a definite slam try, so you would never bother with cue-bids merely to reach game. Sometimes, you can start cue-bidding with a limited hand, but these bids will be below the level of game, simply to show suitability for a slam. Almost always, however, it will be the unlimited hand in the auction that decides to make the move to look for slam, and only that hand is permitted to move above the game level.

A cue-bid shows the ace (sometimes a void) in the suit you name. You are able to show all your controls in this way, other than in the trump suit. Bidding the agreed trump suit is a sign-off manoeuvre, stating that you have no further controls to show partner, or that you are not interested in continuing the slam search.

Let's see some cue-bids in action:

a)

		W	E
W	**E**	1S	3S
♠ K98632	♠ AQ54	4C	4D
♡ AKQ2	♡ 43	4NT	5S
◇ 93	◇ A654	6S	
♣ A	♣ 952		

a) With spades agreed strongly, West could not use Roman Key Card Blackwood immediately as, if East showed one ace, West would not know how to proceed. Before any thought of a slam, he needs to know whether East holds ◇A to stop two quick losers in that suit. He cue-bids 4C and, when East bids 4D to show his control there, West feels confident enough to use Roman Key Card Blackwood. East's 5S response shows two aces and the trump queen, so West can bid 6S with some confidence.

Notice that you continue to show the total number of aces in response to Roman Key Card Blackwood even though you have already shown ◇A by cue-bidding.

b)

		W	E
W	**E**	2C	2D
♠ Q105	♠ AJ43	2H	3H
♡ AKQJ98	♡ 543	4D	4S
◇ AKQ7	◇ 96	5C	5H
♣ -	♣ J972	6H	

b) Following the heart agreement, West wants to know only whether East holds spade controls. He cue-bids 4D and East duly bids 4S confirming ♠A or possibly a void. West continues cue-bidding, this time with 5C, hoping to hear East repeat his spade cue-bid to show ♠K also. However, when East bids 5H, it is a sign-off showing no further controls, and West settles for the small slam.

In what order should you show controls?

Generally, it is best not to cue-bid a void initially, unless you think it is of great use to partner, and you have plenty of trumps with which partner can ruff out his losers in that suit.

Otherwise, the most sensible method of cue-bidding involves combining bidding first the suit in which you are more interested in hearing about partner's second and third round controls, and second picking the order of cue-bids that allows most bidding space. For example:

W

♠ AK
♡ AK7532
◇ 43
♣ A86

N	E	S	W
–	–	–	1H
NB	3H	NB	?

Many players would cue-bid 3S now, because it appears to keep the bidding lower. But there are two good reasons not to do this. Firstly, you want your partner to know that it is in clubs which you most want to hear further infor-mation. Secondly, when you are planning to cue-bid twice – if you hear the right information from partner after the first cue-bid – you should work out which order of cue-bids will be more economical *in the long run*.

Note that if you miss out a suit with your initial cue-bid you are *not* denying a first round control in that suit. You are merely organising your cue-bids to suit what you anticipate will be the subsequent auction. Obviously, if you studiously ignore the same suit subsequently, it is a clear message to partner – and to the opposition – that you are not rich in high cards in that suit.

In the above example, you are hoping to hear partner cue-bid 4D. If he does not, you will probably just settle for game – so let's analyse the possible auctions:

a)

W	E
1H	3H
3S	4D
5C	

b)

W	E
1H	3H
4C	4D
4S	

a) Bidding the spade control initially appeared more space-saving, but has resulted in your having to move to the 5-level to show your second control.

b) Whereas, now you are still at the 4-level, allowing your partner to show his ♣K with a cue-bid of 5C or, possibly, even to bid 4NT.

So, where economy of space is not an issue, opt for the suit in which you want partner to co-operate if possible. Otherwise, keep an eye on how you foresee the cue-bidding auction progressing in the event of partner making the noises you are hoping to hear.

Cue-bidding first and second round controls

As with Blackwood, you will check to see that you have first round controls in all the suits and then, if you have, you can ask about second, or even third, round controls. Generally, by the time you start asking for kings, it will be because you are certain of the small slam, and you wish to investigate the grand.

W	E
♠ AK6532	♠ Q984
♡ A	♡ J54
◇ KQ2	◇ A8
♣ A98	♣ KQJ5

W	E
2D	2H
2S	3S
4C	4D
4H	5C
5D	6C
7S	

Playing Weak 2s East-West find their strong spade agreement, and cue-bid ♣A, ◇A and ♡A. East, holding a very strong hand opposite a Strong 2 in spades, now shows his ♣K by cue-bidding the suit a second time (5C). West is now looking only at a club loser, and can attempt to persuade East to show either ♡K if he holds it, or even ♣Q. Although cue-bidding to show third round controls is rare, East has such good trick taking potential in clubs, he is worth one more cue-bid. West need have no qualms about bidding 7S (or 7NT at duplicate).

You may feel that East is making a big leap of faith to cue-bid at the 6-level, but he must trust West. West has chosen to cue-bid clubs first and that means that he is interested in hearing about East's high cards in that suit. And clearly West is committed to a small slam when he cue-bids 5D, or he would have signed off in 5S, so even if 6C is not what he wants to hear, he can settle for 6S. Finally, East should not worry about his trumps. West has shown a 6-card suit, so East's 4-card support is one more than West will be expecting. Besides, West has taken control of the auction and must be trusted to hold good enough trumps not to be worried about that suit.

Showing a second round control immediately

This is a relatively rare, but completely acceptable practice. The way to avoid partnership angst is to remember that it is fine to lie about which aces you hold, but not about the total number in your hand.

W

♠ K8
♡ A753
◇ 432
♣ KJ86

N	E	S	W
–	1H	NB	3H
NB	3S	NB	?

Bid 4C. You have an incredibly suitable hand for a slam – all aces and kings. Also, your ♣K looks fabulous now that partner has shown you ♠A. To sign off in 4H would be incredibly weedy, so you should definitely cue-bid 4C. This is not dangerous at all. Partner has made a mild slam try with his 3S cue-bid and you are co-operating. If he now asks for aces with Roman Key Card Blackwood, you will show him one, and he is unlikely to be disappointed that it is the ace of trumps rather than ♣A.

If you hold no aces in your hand, it would be most unwise to cue-bid kings immediately, because you are likely to end up at the 6-level with two aces missing. However, as long as you have an ace to spare – it will usually be the ace of trumps – you are quite safe to co-operate in partner's cue-bidding sequence.

As you become more confident with your cue-bidding, you will discover that there are times when you can cue-bid second round controls, even without a compensating ace. But here, we are trying to adopt a reasonably accurate method which will avoid too many disasters, for it is those which cause the unnecessary stress at the table.

Finally, a word of caution. Do not sit there imagining that your partner might be holding exactly the right cards for a slam. If you need him to hold one key card, and you can investigate this at a safe level, fine. If you need him to hold three perfect cards, take no risks whilst investigating, because the odds against him holding all the cards you need are too remote. In the long run, you will gain by bidding solid games and safe, simple slams. The number of gains you will make from bidding complex slams will be relatively small and, if you overreach too often, you will start to lose a lot of points at rubber bridge or teams of four.

QUANTITATIVE BIDDING

When bidding No-trumps, points take on greater importance and, when partner's last bid has shown a possible range of three or four points, it may be vital to ascertain at which end of the spectrum your partner's hand lies. To this end, Quantitative bids ask simply, are you minimum or maximum for your NT bid?

Most pairs already play Quantitative bids, but usually only in response to opening bids of 1NT and 2NT:

- 1NT or 2NT – 4NT asks opener to pass if he is minimum, and bid 6NT if maximum.

If you are maximum however, just leaping to 6NT seems a bit of a waste of space. Experts apply all sorts of meanings to all the bids in between, but I will make one suggestion that I think is the most useful of all. If you accept the slam invitation, and your hand contains a good quality 5-card suit, you should jump to that suit at the 6-level rather than 6NT. This offers partner a choice of slams. You may argue that at duplicate, you will want to be in 6NT even if it is not the best possible spot, but at teams or rubber bridge, the *safest* slam is unquestionably where you want to be.

Even more important than this is how often you utilize quantitative raises. These bids really are far too useful to reserve merely for responses to opening bids. There are many occasions when the strength of partner's opening 1NT bid or rebid of NTs at higher levels will be the only deciding factor for a slam, and Blackwood – of any kind – will not be useful.

For this reason, the experts all play that 4NT is *always* a quantitative raise – not Blackwood of any kind – when their partner has opened 1NT or rebid NTs, unless a trump suit has been clearly agreed.

Each of the following examples applies equally opposite a 2NT opening:

a)

W	E
1NT	2C
2S	4NT

b)

W	E
1NT	2C
2S	4C
4S	4NT

a) 4NT is quantitative because, if you hold a 19/20-count with a 4-card heart suit, what else can you bid to investigate a possible 6NT?

b) If you have a good hand with spade support, all you need to do is to make a cue-bid (here the 4C bid is a cue-bid showing ♣A) and then bid 4NT over partner's sign-off or cue-bid, and this will clearly be Roman Key Card Blackwood.

The same principles apply when playing transfers – if no fit has been agreed, 4NT is quantitative; if a fit has been agreed, 4NT is Roman Key Card Blackwood.

c)

W	E
1NT	2D
2H	4NT

d)

W	E
1NT	2D
3C	4NT

c) 4NT is quantitative, showing a hand of 19/20 points, including a 5-card heart suit. The 1NT opener can pass, bid 6H or 6NT.

d) 4NT is Roman Key Card Blackwood because the opener has broken the transfer, agreeing the suit, and showing a particularly suitable hand for playing with hearts as trumps.

4NT is still quantitative when partner rebids NTs:

e)	W	E		f)	W	E
	1D	1S			1S	2H
	1NT	4NT			3NT	4NT

e) Although the opener's rebid range is officially 15-16 points, we should all know that the real range is from a very good 14 points to a truly lousy 17 points. For this reason it makes sense to play 4NT as quantitative.

f) Here, in Acol, the range is 17-20 points, and a quantitative raise is vital to distinguish between the two extremes.

Although Quantitative Bidding may seem unnatural to some of you, it is an agreement well worth coming to with your partner. You will find that it avoids many agonizing decisions, whilst still leaving you with the opportunity to use Blackwood by cue-bidding first, and then subsequently bidding 4NT.

EXCLUSION BLACKWOOD

One further slam manoeuvre is worth examining, which although a rare bird indeed, is easy to learn and remember and will save you having to make a potentially very expensive guess. This gadget is widely used by expert pairs, but rarely adopted by club players.

When a suit has been agreed in a strong sequence, an unnecessary jump to the 5-level (or the 4-level when the 3-level would have been a cue-bid) activates "Exclusion Blackwood". For example:

W	E
1S	3S
5C	

or

W	E
2C	2D
2H	3H
5D	

also

W	E
1H	3H
4S	

In each case, the jump to five of a new suit (the final bid above) asks, how many aces *excluding* this suit do you hold? The intention is to find an ace-count in suits other than the one in which you are *void*. This may be especially useful when your hand contains a void and not the ace of trumps. This type of hand would normally require cue-bids and Roman Key Card Blackwood, and there may well not be room to investigate everything.

The responses are graduated: the next suit up shows no aces; the next one ace, the next two aces, etc.

This hand actually came up in a simultaneous pairs competition a few years back, and must have proved a nightmare for pairs not playing Exclusion Blackwood. For those acquainted with the convention, the grand slam was a doddle:

W	E
♠ KQJ98	♠ A754
♡ KQJ43	♡ A5
◇ -	◇ 9863
♣ KQ8	♣ A72

W	E
1S	3S
5D	6C
7S	

West's jump to 5D asked East how many aces he held outside the diamond suit. The next suit up, 5H, would have showed none; the next suit up, 5S, one ace; 5NT, two aces and the actual response of 6C showed all three aces outside of diamonds. Now, 7S was easy.

SLAM BIDDING:
KEY FACTS

- Roman Key Card Blackwood and Cue-bidding are the mainstays of slam bidding.
- Exclusion Blackwood is an advanced gadget which, whilst powerful, occurs only infrequently.

Because slams don't crop up that often, you and your partner will need to practise these new conventions so that you feel confident to use them in competition. One method is to remove the twos, threes, fours and fives from a deck of cards, and deal you and your partner a hand each. You will get plenty of games and plenty of slams.

The section below completes the bidding part of your convention card.

SLAM CONVENTIONS	Meaning of responses	Action over interference
RKCB	Trump K = 5th ace 5C=0/3 aces 5D=1/4 aces 5H=2 aces; no trump Q 5S=2 aces + trump Q	DOPI
EXCLUSION BLACKWOOD		

Other Conventions

a) Lebensohl in response to a reverse; in response to T.O. double which forced 3-level reply,
b) 4th suit forcing,
c) Unassuming Cue-bids.

PART FIVE
HIGH LEVEL COMPETITIVE BIDDING

I N a competitive auction the choice between bidding on, doubling, and passing, is one of the toughest in the game.

In Larry Cohen's landmark book, *To Bid or Not To Bid*, he brilliantly explains the Law of Total Tricks, which extends our Total Trumps Principle into the realms of all four hands. It is a complex and absorbing read. Any player truly interested in improving his competitive bidding should make Larry Cohen's book the next on their list.

Here, we will finish with a look at the basic principles behind the Law of Total Tricks, so that we can begin to apply it in high-level competitive situations.

First, and most importantly however, are the guiding principles to which, it seems, even some of the most experienced players seem oblivious. As everyone seems to prefer to bid on rather than to defend – a policy which is far more often wrong than right – we will concentrate on reasons to defend.

GUIDING PRINCIPLES OF HIGH LEVEL COMPETITIVE BIDDING

The 5-level is for the opponents.

This is a well-known piece of advice, too rarely heeded.

Basically, if your opponents were heading for a quiet 4H or 4S game, and your competitive bidding drives them to the 5-level, you should never continue to compete to the 5-level yourself. By pushing them one level higher than they wished, you have applied enough pressure. If they make their contract, you have lost nothing; if they fail, you may have swung a game score in your favour.

The nightmare scenario is if you bid to the 5-level, go down doubled, and lose 500 or 800, and then find that they couldn't make their own 5-level contract. If you don't recognize this scenario from your own games, you possess either excellent judgment, or a selective memory . . .

The underlying rule about pre-emption holds good. Having pre-empted, don't bid on. Barrage your opponents, then leave them be. Put it another way. We all know how tough it is to make high-level decisions. Just put your opponents in the position where they have to make the final guess.

Finally, as you will see in the section on the Law of Total Tricks, the entire deal will have to be extraordinarily distributional to produce lots of tricks for each side. Particularly at rubber bridge and teams of four, if you don't think that the distribution is extraordinary, with ten and eleven card trump fits for each side – don't even consider the 5-level.

If you hold two cards or fewer in partner's first suit, a misfit is developing: if you hold a misfit, defend.

These thoughts should echo around your head throughout the bidding. In an uncontested auction, if your partnership has no fit, your aim is to keep the bidding low. In a competitive auction, your aim should be to pass.

I explained this to a very experienced player recently, who looked askance that I should be teaching him anything so basic. Yet, this was the very next hand:

W
♠ 532
♡ AQ1086
◇ 3
♣ J864

N	E	S	W
–	1D	1H	?

Without a thought, in he waded with 1NT. Within a few moments his partner, who was 6-5 in diamonds and spades, found himself in 4S doubled. Trumps were led, diamonds broke 5-1, and nothing in West's hand proved remotely useful. East-West lost 800 points on a part-score hand. What a waste!

This hand starts as a decent 7-count. When partner opens 1D it gets worse, much worse. Then, South over-calls 1H and the hand suddenly becomes fabulous news – in defence. Why then should West want to bid?

Playing Negative Doubles, if West had passed, East might have been able to re-open with a double, which West could have passed out for penalties. Even with part-ner holding a 6-5 hand, East-West could have stopped in 2S and emerged relatively unscathed. But, the moment West bid, he was telling his partner that the news from the auction was good, and that he felt his side should be playing the hand.

W
♠ 5
♡ K86
◇ AQ8643
♣ 964

N	E	S	W
–	1S	2H	?

Here is another typical problem. To me, this is easy because, the moment my partner opened the suit in which I was singleton, I knew that we would have to put the brakes on the auction. When my RHO intervenes, I am delighted to take the opportunity of passing. If my partner re-opens with a double, I can get excited; if he re-bids spades – which is far more likely – I can pass again, and he will be pleasantly surprised by my high cards.

Of course, if partner holds the perfect hand, with six great spades, a club shortage and ◊K, we will miss game. But, as I have said before, and am happy to repeat:

> *partner never has the perfect hand – especially when you have considered the possibility that he might.*

The bottom line is that missing the odd game is a small price to pay for avoiding hundreds of bad high level contracts on misfits.

> *If you hold high cards in your partner's suits, bid on; if you hold high cards in the opponent's suits, or in unbid suits, defend.*

In these two examples the auctions are identical:

a) W
- ♠ Q432
- ♡ 532
- ◊ K74
- ♣ 864

b) W
- ♠ 65
- ♡ K108
- ◊ 9843
- ♣ Q1092

N	E	S	W
–	1D	1H	NB
2H	2S	3H	?

a) Bid 3S. All your points are concentrated in partner's two suits and, considering that you have promised nothing, you have a great hand. If partner cannot make 3S, then your opponents must be cold for 3H.

b) Pass. 4D must be very unlikely to be right, and with none of your points in partner's suits, you should be keen to defend. For example, partner probably holds a singleton heart, so your ♡K may not contribute a trick as dummy, but will score in defence. Similarly in clubs, partner may well be doubleton, so ♣Q will not help. Again, in defence, it is very likely to score a trick.

At higher levels, observe how a pure fit – with the points fitting as well as the suit length – can produce so many extra tricks:

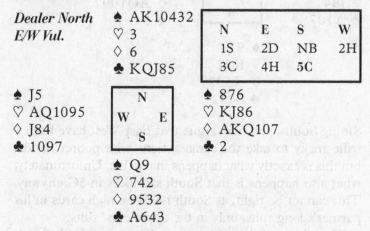

Dealer North
E/W Vul.

North

♠ AK10432
♡ 3
◇ 6
♣ KQJ85

N	E	S	W
1S	2D	NB	2H
3C	4H	5C	

West

♠ J5
♡ AQ1095
◇ J84
♣ 1097

South

♠ 876
♡ KJ86
◇ AKQ107
♣ 2

♠ Q9
♡ 742
◇ 9532
♣ A643

North's bidding strongly suggests his 6-5 shape as, with just a strong 5-4 shape, he might have chosen to double at his second turn. South happily bids 5C over East's jump to game, because he realises that all his points are concentrated in his partner's long suits. Both 4H and 5C (and, indeed 4S) make because each side enjoys a double fit, with their points concentrated in their own suits. Each of the four suits is very pure – that is to say, it is headed by at least the top three honours – so the suits produce tricks automatically, with no need to ruff out losers to establish the suit.

If we look at a very similar deal, with the high cards not concentrated in partner's long suits, we will see a significant reduction in the trick-taking potential of both partnerships.

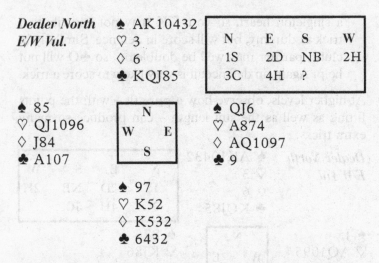

Dealer North
E/W Vul.

♠ AK10432
♡ 3
◇ 6
♣ KQJ85

	N	E	S	W
	1S	2D	NB	2H
	3C	4H	?	

♠ 85
♡ QJ1096
◇ J84
♣ A107

♠ QJ6
♡ A874
◇ AQ1097
♣ 9

♠ 97
♡ K52
◇ K532
♣ 6432

Sitting South, you may argue that East-West have been a trifle frisky to take the same actions with poorer hands, but this is exactly what happens in real life. Unfortunately, what also happens is that South sacrifices in 5C anyway. This cannot be right, as South holds no high cards in his partner's long suits, only in the opponents' suits.

This time, neither side can make game: North-South can muster only nine tricks in spades, or ten in clubs, and East-West only nine in hearts. Everyone has the same number of points and trumps, but the potential for tricks is limited by the lack of pure fits in each of the suits. As South, you are the one to make the last decision and, thankfully, you can see your values in the opponents' suits and can decide to defend.

North may decide to bid again – he does have a hand which looks most unsuitable for defence. However, he has shown his shape and playing strength, and you have chosen not to act. If he does bid on, at least he cannot claim that you encouraged him.

Having noted the position of your high cards, don't forget that you must have length in partner's suits as well.

Without trump length, you will always be short of tricks and, more importantly, if your values are concentrated in short holdings, these are ideal for defence:

Dealer West
E/W Vul.

	♠ 1032				
	♡ —	**N**	**E**	**S**	**W**
	◇ AQ1097	–	–	–	1H
	♣ K10987	2NT	4H	?	

♠ A7	**N**	♠ KQ86
♡ KJ953	**W E**	♡ AQ106
◇ J84	**S**	◇ 653
♣ QJ3		♣ 54

♠ J954
♡ 8742
◇ K2
♣ A62

Sitting South, how tempted are you to bid 5C? You do hold excellent cards in your partner's suits, and your heart length suggests shortage opposite you. But, even if your minor suit holdings help to make ten tricks in those suits, you will still fail at the 5-level. That would be fine if East-West could make ten tricks in hearts, but can they? If your minor suits are as solid as you hope that they are, surely you can take enough tricks there to defeat 4H? After all, you only hold seven diamonds and eight clubs between you – not long enough that you suspect that your opponents hold singletons.

In fact, your opponents are two down in 4H after a minor suit lead; even if partner leads a spade, they cannot succeed. That is excellent news for your side – unless you bid 5C...

Unless you have a double fit (two eight card fits or longer) don't compete at the 5-level without a 10-card trump fit.

Picture the entire distribution, and recognize your side's defensive holdings in your opponents' suit(s).

This is a detail from the preceding pieces of advice. Here, look only at your holdings in your opponents' suit:

W

♠ Q943
♡ Q107
◇ 4
♣ 86432

N	E	S	W
1D	1S	2H	3S
4H	NB	NB	?

Many players would reason that, as they hold three hearts, their partner will hold a singleton. Together with their own singleton diamond, this means that a big cross-ruff is on the cards, and 4S will be a good sacrifice. This is reasonable thinking, but it is not deep enough.

a) If partner holds a singleton heart – which is probable – will your ♡Q be of any help in playing the hand? Of course not. But, in defence, it is very likely to score a trick. Even if partner holds a doubleton heart, your ♡Q won't score playing the hand, but will in defence.

b) Partner did not bid 4S himself, suggesting that he only holds a 5-card spade suit. This means that you have only nine spades between you, and that you can make up to two tricks in defence in that suit.

c) If he also holds a singleton heart, he is long in clubs and diamonds. If he has any length in diamonds, this is excellent for defence, as he is sitting over the opening diamond bidder, and may well scoop up tricks there.

Let's construct a hand for him:

W		E
♠ Q943		♠ AJ1085
♡ Q107		♡ 5
◇ 4		◇ QJ86
♣ 86432		♣ A95

If the spade finesse is right, we will only be one down. But we are likely to be able to take *at least* one trick in each suit defending against 4H, so our sacrifice will be a phantom, losing us points on a hand where our aggressive barrage to 3S had put us in a winning position, having pushed them too high.

The key to realising that pass was a winner lay in identifying our defensive holdings. Notice that in 4S, our ♡Q is waste-paper, as are partner's ◇QJ, whereas in defence, each holding is likely to make a trick.

The defensive holdings to look out for are the queens, jacks and tens in the opponents' suits, because if these are opposite shortages in partner's hand, they will be of little use if your side is declaring.

HELPING PARTNER TO JUDGE THE SITUATION

In some cases, it will be right to bid on. When you feel that you have the sort of hand with which you will not want to defend, the least you can do is to involve your partner in the decision making process.

As you become more experienced, you can agree all kinds of expert arrangements, but here are two very simple suggestions for you and your partner, which are, hopefully, easy to understand and remember.

1. Showing extra distribution

In the same way that fit jumps help partner to judge whether to bid on, so you should inform your partner of extra distribution, even at high levels, so that he can judge whether to bid on, pass, or double.

W	N	E	S	W
♠ AQJ103				1S
♡ AQ1072	—	—	—	
◊ 4	2D	2S	4D	?
♣ A6				

Bid 4H. Clearly, you want to be in 4S on this hand. However, you must be prepared in case North-South sacrifice in 5D. To this end, instead of bidding 4S now, you should bid 4H. This shows your second suit, and will help partner to judge what to bid over North's possible 5D bid. For example, if partner holds:

♠ K94
♡ KJ53
◊ 62
♣ 8542

you will want to be in 5S, and you can expect him to bid it. Whereas, if he holds:

♠ K94
♡ 63
♢ Q102
♣ J9532

you do not want to compete at the 5-level, and you can expect your partner to double (or at least pass) when the opponents bid 5D. Whatever might still have happened to 5S, 5D doubled will make you a good deal richer.

This leads us on to the final piece of guidance for high level bidding.

2. Passing, doubling, and bidding on over opponents' sacrifice.

I propose a very simple set of guidelines which are easy to learn and to put into practice at the table. Bear in mind that with competitive bidding becoming ever more aggressive, you will be faced with these types of situation more and more frequently.

Here are the ground rules:

- If you and your partner bid to a game which you expect to make and your opponents sacrifice, you should never leave them to play in their contract undoubled. It is incumbent upon one member of your partnership to double or to bid on.

- When the opponent sacrifices, bear in mind that your gut instinct should be to double and take the money. However, there is more science to it than that. If you are the first member of your partnership to speak, you have three options to help your partnership come to the right decision: pass, double or bid on. I have given an example of each below.

a) Pass. This indicates that your hand contains no significant factors which can help you to decide whether you should be doubling the opposition, or bidding on in your agreed suit. This pass is forcing – when the bidding reaches your partner, he will have to double, or bid on.

W

	N	E	S	W
♠ KJ43	–	1S	2D	3S
♡ Q72				
◇ 4	4D	4S	5D	NB
♣ A6432				

It is not clear on this hand whether you would be happier in 5S or defending 5D doubled. As far as you are concerned, your partner may well hold a long spade suit and a secondary fit in clubs or hearts with you. If, on the other hand, he holds ◇Q10x, he will be very happy to double, and that will be the right decision.

b) Double. This is not a clearcut penalty double – although you may wish that it was on some occasions. Double simply indicates that you do not wish to continue bidding on and, within the context of the bidding, you feel that your hand is best suited to defence. It does not promise a trump trick.

W

	N	E	S	W
♠ KJ43	–	1S	2D	3S
♡ 107				
◇ QJ6	4D	4S	5D	Dbl
♣ A643				

Holding ◇QJx, opposite what is very likely to be a singleton in partner's hand, should immediately tip you off that this is a hand which you should be defending, rather than trying to make eleven tricks. Notice also that here you hold only four clubs, which would make a secondary fit with partner much less useful to you.

c) Bid on. This should be a very rare option, because it is a unilateral decision, preventing your partner from doubling. Such a decision should only be made with extra length in your trump suit, or a second suit that offers a chance of a double fit.

W		N	E	S	W
♠ KQJ9432		–	–	–	1S
♡ 7					
◇ 932		2D	4S	5D	5S
♣ AQ					

Your partner has made a weak distributional raise to 4S, and you hold seven trumps of your own. It may still be wrong to bid 5S, but your hand offers so little defensive potential, it may be your side who needs to sacrifice. So, this is a two-edged sword. You may make 5S, or you may fail by a trick or two when the opposition were making 5D.

I have to say though, I still feel uneasy bidding on. The words "the 5-level is for the opponents" are ringing in my ears . . .

3. If you are the last to bid, there are several options:

a) If your partner doubled the opponents, you should virtually always stand it, even if you opened light originally. This is an important element. Once you decide to open the bidding on a weak hand, you must not later try to rescue your partner from high-level penalty doubles. If you make an informed decision to open the bidding, you must respect that decision later on. If it turns out to be wrong, you can change the way you open your hands in future. The key is that your partner may have the extra values you lacked – he will not be pleased if you pull his "double of the century". . .

If you are much more distributional than your bidding has suggested, or you have a second suit which will definitely provide tricks in the play, you might consider bidding on. However, this will be a rare occurrence.

b) If your partner passed, you are now forced to bid on or double. Your inclination should be to double, unless you really believe that you have a good chance to make the contract you are being pushed into. A strong second suit in your hand, which you have not had time to show, might be justification for continuing.

W

♠ AKQ43
♡ Q107
♢ 42
♣ A64

N	E	S	W
–	–	–	1S
2D	3S	4D	4S
5D	NB	NB	Dbl

You bid 4S quite happily to make, but you have no reason to continue to the 5-level. The fact that your partner passed has indicated that he has a standard raise to 3S, and that means that his hand will contain some defensive tricks in hearts and clubs. So you double.

c) Again, your partner passes.

W

♠ AKQ43
♡ 107
♢ 4
♣ AK432

N	E	S	W
–	–	–	1S
2D	3S	4D	4S
5D	NB	NB	5S

The opponents have certainly spoiled your fun on this hand. You might have a slam on here, but you were prevented from investigating it, and now your solid game has been threatened. However, partner's pass over 5D suggests that he does not have a defensive trick in diamonds, and that his points are therefore concentrated in the other suits. That makes eleven tricks in spades a good chance, whereas 5D may get out for a meagre penalty. So this is where you bid on.

Obviously all these decisions will be influenced by vulnerability. Usually, you will face 4 and 5-level decisions when your opponents are not vulnerable, and bidding on seems more tempting. However, try to remember that although it is frustrating to score only +100 doubling your opponents' sacrifice when you had a cold game, it is more frustrating to score -100 by bidding on. In other words, if +100 is the best score available now, it is no use bemoaning the fact that you might have had a bigger score moments ago.

If you find these decisions tough, then you are just like the rest of us, and you realise pretty quickly that even the best players make the wrong decision. One final factor that will help to guide you to the right conclusion is the Law of Total Tricks. This understanding is used by every top bridge player in the world to a greater or lesser degree. Although it is not perfect, it is extraordinarily accurate, even in the most basic form described here. It takes a little dedication to apply it, but it is well worth the effort.

THE LAW OF TOTAL TRICKS

On every hand of bridge, the total number of tricks available is equal – or very close to – the total number of cards in each side's longest suit. The distribution of high cards is irrelevant for, the more suitably they lie for one side, the less well placed they are for the other. So, obviously, where the high cards are located is of significance to each partnership, but not to the total number of tricks available on any given hand.

Let's illustrate the principle with an example:

Dealer East ♠ Q32
E/W Vul. ♡ QJ92
        ♢ 98
        ♣ A854

N	E	S	W
–	1D	1S	2D
2S	3D	?	

♠ 754	**N**	♠ J9
♡ 108	**W** **E**	♡ A764
♢ KJ64	**S**	♢ AQ1073
♣ QJ97		♣ K10

        ♠ AK1086
        ♡ K53
        ♢ 52
        ♣ 632

As a devotee of the Total Trumps Principle, which is derived from the Law of Total Tricks, our instinct sitting South would be to pass, realising that with eight trumps between us, we had reached the top limit for our competition. However, the Law of Total Tricks suggests that we should bid on. Here are the reasons:

We know that we hold eight spades between us. From the auction, we can assume that East-West hold nine diamonds – East certainly has five and it would be unusual for West to raise a minor suit without four. Working on that assumption, we know that there are 17 trumps (obviously only one suit can be trumps, but we don't know which will be trumps yet, so we can call both sides' longest suit "trumps"). This means that there will be 17 tricks available on the hand. We do not know how many each side will make but, again, if we assume that East bid 3D to make, he is expecting to make nine tricks, and that will leave eight tricks for our side. With this vulnerability, it would be well worth our bidding 3S and failing by a trick, even if doubled, to stop the opposition making their 3D. Of course, it may be that our side will make the nine tricks, and the opponents were only making eight. In that case, we make our contract. Either way, it should be right for South to bid 3S.

Try moving around the high cards, without changing the number of diamonds and spades each partnership holds, and you will find there are still 17 tricks available. The location of high cards simply does not matter, only the number of trumps.

Of course, you don't always know how many trumps you and your partner hold between you, let alone how many the opposition have. But you can usually make a decent guess, and that is often enough. Sometimes, the arithmetic of the scoring will make it worth taking an extra risk at duplicate pairs, whereas at teams or rubber bridge, the possible margin of error might prove too costly. However, application of the Law of Total Tricks will prove hugely productive at all forms of the game. Let's try this out on another hand:

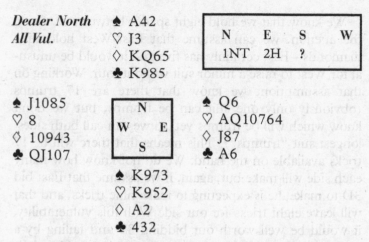

Dealer North
All Vul.

♠ A42
♡ J3
◇ KQ65
♣ K985

N	E	S	W
1NT	2H	?	

♠ J1085
♡ 8
◇ 10943
♣ QJ107

♠ Q6
♡ AQ10764
◇ J87
♣ A6

♠ K973
♡ K952
◇ A2
♣ 432

This is a familiar situation. Sitting South, partner opens a Weak NT, RHO overcalls, and you have enough points to want to act, but not enough to try for game. Should you pass quietly and hopefully collect +100? Or should you try a speculative 2S, or even 2NT? Or should you double?

The last option becomes clear-cut when you analyse the evidence. Firstly, we know that East-West hold no more than seven hearts, because partner must have two for his 1NT opening. So, even if we only think of the TTP, we know that East-West are too high already – at the eight trick level with only seven trumps.

Taking the thinking further, we can apply the Law of Total Tricks. East-West have seven trumps in hearts, we have no more than an eight card trump fit, possibly in spades, maybe in clubs, if partner opened with a 5-card club suit. Either way, there is a maximum of 15 trumps on this hand. As we hold the clear majority of points, we can expect to be making the majority of those tricks. Say we can make eight tricks, that leaves the opponents with only seven. At this vulnerability, even one down doubled for +200, gives us a score that will beat any part-score that we can make.

As you can see, our assumptions were wrong. We do not hold an 8-card fit. The maximum fit we have is a 7-card spade fit. So, the real total number of trumps is 14. But this is even better news for us. It means that if we can make a part-score, the opponents have even fewer tricks.

In fact, the opponents can make only six tricks in 2H doubled, giving us +500 when making anything more than 1NT looks tough.

Let's see whether the Law of Total Tricks can help us with high level decisions.

Dealer West   ♠ AK87
Love All   ♡ K654
                    ◇ 6
                    ♣ QJ52

N	E	S	W
–	–	–	1D
Dbl	4D	?	

♠ Q2   ♠ 10643
♡ Q108   ♡ 97
◇ AKJ8   ◇ Q10742
♣ K1076   ♣ 94

                    ♠ J95
                    ♡ AJ32
                    ◇ 953
                    ♣ A83

South would have faced a tough choice between 2H and 3H had East passed but, now, should he bid 4H? The Law of Total Tricks will solve the dilemma. East-West hold at least nine diamonds, possibly ten, although that would leave North with a diamond void, and he might have preferred to overcall a 5-card suit originally rather than doubling. Let's assume nine diamonds then. We almost certainly have an 8-card heart fit. So, there are 17 trumps. If we can make ten tricks in 4H, they have only seven tricks in 4D doubled. I would rather have +500 than +420, so double looks favourite.

But what if we can't make ten tricks in 4H. If we only make nine tricks, we will go down in 4H, scoring -50. However, East-West will only have eight tricks, so they will still fail by two tricks in 4D doubled. So, now 4D scores +300, against -50.

However the tricks are divided, the Law of Total Tricks tells us we should double, and not bid 4H.

The first scenario was correct. We can't make 4H, and they are minus three in 4D.

Like the Total Trumps Principle, the Law of Total Tricks is based on the assumption that everyone is playing and defending the hands perfectly, which is tough to do even at World Championship level. The principles of the Law of Total Tricks, however, are completely sound and will help you to make the right sort of decisions.

This is the beginner's outline. There are adjustments and understandings to study and learn. They are quite tough, but they are well worth the trouble. The next time you play a hand, keep the cards, and analyse it according to the Law of Total Tricks. You will find that it will be accurate to within one trick on the vast majority of hands.

To conclude, here are three common situations, with some instant guidance from the Law of Total Tricks:

1. **When there are 16 trumps** (usually when you both have an 8-card fit) **do not bid at the 3-level if your opponents are already there**. If they can make nine tricks, you will only have seven tricks – two off, doubled, is too expensive.

2. **When there are 17 trumps, you should compete at the 3-level.** If your opponents can make nine tricks, you are making eight for one off. If your opponents can only make eight tricks, you are making nine tricks in your 3-level contract.

3. To sacrifice at the 5-level, over the opponents' 4-level contract, there will need to be at least 19 trumps – assuming equal vulnerability. You should hold at least ten trumps to consider bidding at the 5-level in competition.

HIGH LEVEL COMPETITIVE BIDDING: KEY FACTS

However experienced a player you are, high level competitive bidding is still a tough proposition. However, the same considerations apply at high levels as for low levels, and the main guidelines here echo the basic principles outlined in Part 1.

- Do not compete at the 5-level without 10 trumps or a known double fit.

- Recognise a misfit, when partner is bidding suits in which you are short, and do not encourage him by supporting, even at a late stage in the auction. Plan to defend.

- If your high cards lie in partner's long suits, be more inclined to bid on; if they are scattered around your hand, consider defending.

- Look for defensive holdings, such as Qx and Q10x in the opponents' suits. These will be useless to your partner, but will make tricks in defence.

Help partner to judge the situation:

- In a competitive auction, show extra distribution by bidding out the full shape of your hand, even once you have agreed a suit with partner.

- If there is a double fit, you will make more tricks. If both sides have a big double fit, it will generally pay to bid on, rather than defending.

Apply the Law of Total Tricks to establish whether there is a high enough trump total to warrant further competition.

A FINAL WORD

I hope that you will adopt many, if not all, of the suggestions in these pages. If you can do this successfully, you will be playing a system powerful enough to cope with most circumstances, yet simple enough to remember under pressure.

However, even if you choose only a few of these innovations, you have, at least, a working knowledge of the type of conventions and the style of bidding you will encounter when you play against other good players.

Partnership confidence, within a relaxed relationship, is the single most important factor in succeeding and enjoying your bridge. As you adopt these innovations, both you and your partner will make mistakes. If you can laugh at them, and realise that this is part of any learning process, then you will succeed. Indeed, one never learns much from one's successes at bridge. The real learning comes from experimenting and failing, and understanding why.

Bob Hamman, the number one ranked player in the world, famously said, "The world's best players are not very good, and everyone else is much worse..." At the very least, I hope that this book will launch you to the top of that latter category and, who knows, maybe into the former one.